The Genre of Autobiography in Victorian Literature

The Genre of Autobiography in Victorian Literature

CLINTON MACHANN

Ann Arbor
THE UNIVERSITY OF MICHIGAN PRESS

Copyright © by the University of Michigan 1994
All rights reserved
Published in the United States of America by
The University of Michigan Press
Manufactured in the United States of America
⊗ Printed on acid-free paper
1997 1996 1995 1994   4 3 2 1

A CIP catalogue record for this book is available from the British Library.

Library of Congress Cataloging-in-Publication Data

Machann, Clinton.
   The genre of autobiography in Victorian literature / Clinton Machann.
      p.   cm.
   Includes bibliographical references (p.   ) and index.
   ISBN 0-472-10565-5 (hardcover : acid-free paper)
   1. English prose literature—19th century—History and criticism.
2. Authors, English—19th century—Biography—History and criticism.
3. Great Britain—History—Victoria, 1837–1901—Historiography.
4. Autobiography. 5. Literary form.   I. Title.
PR788.A9M33   1994
828'.80809492—dc20   94-31065
                                                                              CIP

Acknowledgments

Parts of this book have appeared, in different form, in the following publications: "Ruskin's *Praeterita* and Nineteenth-Century Autobiographical Genre," *English Language Notes* 16 (1978): 156–67; "Gibbon's *Memoirs of My Life* and the Genre of Autobiography in Victorian England," *Prose Studies* 12 (1989): 25–43; "Narrative Structure in Victorian Autobiography," *Nineteenth-Century Prose* 17 (1990): 1–14; "The Function of Illness and Disability in Three Victorian Autobiographies," *A/B: Auto/Biography Studies* 6 (1991): 26–32; "Robert Dale Owen's *Threading My Way* and Victorian Autobiography," *Biography* 15 (1992): 166–78. I am grateful to the editors of the journals for permission to use these materials here.

I also wish to thank David J. DeLaura for reading and commenting on an early draft of this study and the readers for the University of Michigan Press for their detailed and helpful comments. The Department of English and the Interdisciplinary Group for Historical Literary Study at Texas A&M University arranged for teaching-load reductions that helped me complete the manuscript in a timely manner. Finally, I want to recognize the students in my special seminar on Victorian autobiography at Texas A&M in the spring of 1992, whose discussions stimulated my thinking about autobiography in the final stages of this project: Eulail Huffcutt, Don Payne, Karen Riedel, Daniel Rodgers, Clara Speer, and Lillian Wooley.

Contents

Editions of Principal Works — ix

Introduction — 1

1. John Henry Cardinal Newman, *Apologia pro Vita Sua* (1864) — 13
2. John Stuart Mill, *Autobiography* (1873) — 27
3. Robert Dale Owen, *Threading My Way: An Autobiography* (1874) — 37
4. Harriet Martineau, *Autobiography* (1877) — 51
5. Anthony Trollope, *An Autobiography* (1883) — 69
6. John Ruskin, *Praeterita* (1885–89) — 81
7. Charles Darwin, *Autobiography* (1887) — 95
8. Sir Walter Besant, *Autobiography* (1902) — 107
9. Herbert Spencer, *An Autobiography* (1904) — 117
10. Edmund Gosse, *Father and Son* (1907) — 135
11. Francis Galton, *Memories of My Life* (1908) — 145

Conclusion — 159

Notes — 167

Index — 185

Editions of Principal Works Discussed in This Volume

Page references given parenthetically within the text refer to the following titles.

Besant, Walter. *Autobiography of Sir Walter Besant.* New York: Dodd, Mead, 1902.

Darwin, Charles. *The Autobiography of Charles Darwin.* New York: W.W. Norton, 1969.

Galton, Francis. *Memories of My Life.* London: Methuen, 1909.

Gosse, Edmund. *Father and Son.* New York: W. W. Norton, 1963.

Martineau, Harriet. *Harriet Martineau's Autobiography.* 2 vols. 1877; rpt. London: Virago Press, 1983, with an introduction by Gaby Weiner.

Mill, John Stuart. *Autobiography and Other Writings.* Ed. Jack Stillinger. Boston: Houghton Mifflin, 1969.

Newman, John Henry Cardinal. *Apologia pro Vita Sua.* Ed. David J. DeLaura. New York: W. W. Norton, 1968.

Owen, Robert Dale. *Threading My Way: An Autobiography.* 1874; rpt. New York: Augustus M. Kelley, 1967.

Ruskin, John. *Praeterita.* Vol. 35 of *Works*, Library Edition, ed. E. T. Cook and Alexander Wedderburn. London: George Allen, 1904.

Spencer, Herbert. *An Autobiography.* 2 vols. New York: D. Appleton, 1904.

Trollope, Anthony. *An Autobiography.* London: Oxford University Press, 1950.

Introduction

This is a comparative study of eleven autobiographies by British writers who lived their adult lives and published their principal works during the Victorian era, 1832–1901: John Henry Cardinal Newman, *Apologia pro Vita Sua* (1864); John Stuart Mill, *Autobiography* (1873); Robert Dale Owen, *Threading My Way: An Autobiography* (1874); Harriet Martineau, *Autobiography* (1877); Anthony Trollope, *An Autobiography* (1883); John Ruskin, *Praeterita* (1885–89); Charles Darwin, *Autobiography* (1887); Walter Besant, *Autobiography* (1902); Herbert Spencer, *An Autobiography* (1904); Edmund Gosse, *Father and Son* (1907); and Francis Galton, *Memories of My Life* (1908).

My list combines canonical works, recognizable to anyone who is familiar with Victorian literature and culture, with others that are less familiar and that for various reasons help us explore the boundaries of the genre. All of the autobiographies are book length, though some are much longer than others, and all were written by authors who had achieved some degree of fame through their published works, though their fields of interest vary widely. This book has two major purposes. First, it is meant to serve both advanced students and scholars as an introduction to Victorian autobiography. Second, it demonstrates, I hope, that autobiography, at least as it was practiced by the Victorians, can be profitably studied as a nonfiction genre. Like recent critics such as Phillipe Lejeune and Paul John Eakin, who have resisted the poststructuralist critique of the concept of the self, I treat autobiography as a referential art.[1]

I assume that autobiography is a historically determined genre and approach these works with what can be broadly termed a cultural studies methodology. I examine the problematics of self-presentation in the autobiographies and point out, from one point of view, similarities in the strategies employed by this group of writers, and, from another, ways in which the formal characteristics of the genre exert pressure on each writer to conform to certain conventions. These generic conventions are of course linked to other social conventions characteristic of the "age." Most significantly, I hope to show that it is meaningful and fruitful to discuss these nonfiction works as a group, just as it is to discuss, for example, the Victorian novel. Before examining the individual works, however, it is necessary to make basic definitions and clarifications.

The term *autobiography* for "the writing of one's own history" or "the story of one's life written by himself"[2] was accepted rather tentatively by Victorian writers as a group, and the best known autobiographies by Victorian figures during the period running from the mid–nineteenth century through the first decade of the twentieth century often betray an ambivalence toward that term even when it appears in the title. Anthony Trollope called his book an autobiography only because a more suitable term was unavailable (1). He was uncomfortable with the idea of describing his own life and was especially anxious to deny that he was writing in the confessional tradition of Rousseau (365). John Ruskin, among others, used the term interchangeably with *memoirs*, a term now routinely differentiated from the "autobiography proper," described by Roy Pascal in his enormously influential *Design and Truth in Autobiography* as a narrative whose "centre of interest is the self, not the outside world" and that "imposes a pattern on life" and "defines ... a certain consistency of relationship between the self and the outside world."[3] Memoirs are commonly understood to emphasize social and historical data rather than private life. Some authors of works widely read as autobiographies rejected or at least ignored the term. Edmund Gosse rejected it because he claimed that his *Father and Son* was primarily concerned with his father rather than with himself. John Henry Newman chose the term *apologia* as appropriate to his peculiar rhetorical purpose.

The truth is that most of the works that have been classified traditionally as Victorian autobiographies contain at least some components of the apology and of res gestae memoirs or reminiscences, and many of them contain sections that could be described as travelogues, criticism, annotated bibliographies, theoretical and philosophical essays, and various other modes of writing as well. Still, current usage has made *autobiography* the only available term for us to use, and I hope to show that even Trollope and the other Victorian autobiographers who were uncomfortable with the term were writing within a coherent set of generic conventions that were nevertheless flexible enough to accommodate all these different modes of writing. A. O. J. Cockshut insists that "[a]utobiography and memoirs may be mixed in the same book, and sometimes on the same page, but they are still theoretically distinct";[4] however, it seems reasonable to allow for the "impurity" of the genre (as we do for the novel), which is made up of books, not isolated passages.

However, in recent decades, literary scholars have quarreled about definitions of autobiography and about whether it can or should be studied as a genre at all.[5] For this reason I will explain in some detail my theoretical assumptions. As a working definition of autobiography I will adopt one that is more specific than the one given above, that of Lejeune, whose theoretical and descriptive work on the autobiography in France has become well known in recent years. According to him, an autobiography is a "[r]etrospective prose narrative written by a real person concerning his own existence, where the focus is his individual life, in particular the story of his personality."[6] Although this may seem to be a straightforward definition, it is in fact based on some fairly controversial assumptions and apparently would not be accepted by several recent scholars who have written on the subject of Victorian autobiography, as will be seen from the discussion below. Nevertheless, in the following explication of Lejeune's definition, I will attempt to explain why I find it to be a valid and useful one.[7]

Let us first consider the initial phrase "retrospective prose narrative." If the autobiography is retrospective, then it cannot be confused with the journal or the diary or with a collection of letters, though these genres are sometimes lumped together, along with biography, in the general category of life writing. Gerard Manley Hopkins's *Journal* is not an autobiography because it incorporates multiple individual entries written at various points in time, entries that focus on various subjects according to the immediate interest of the day. Though the reader may note themes and motifs that recur throughout the *Journal*, there is no controlling retrospective point of view. More to the point, perhaps, this same generalization is true of the journals, diaries, and letters of the Victorian women whose works are often contrasted to the autobiographies of Victorian men.[8] If these works deserve more study than they have previously received from literary scholars, it is because they are representative of genres that have not been adequately studied; however, this does not mean that we should confuse them with autobiographies. Diaries and journals are most often intended as private documents—not for publication—and we see that Lejeune's definition is most apt for published works.

It is a commonplace that some autobiographies contain letters or portions of diaries or journals, to verify statements and events which would otherwise depend entirely on the memory of the author—Victorian autobiographers routinely use letters in this way—or to illustrate a "typical day" or week in one's life, as Spencer does, in considerable (sometimes wearisome) detail. Routinely, the reader is told or simply assumes that such documents are used by the autobiographer as source materials, so they may be said to constitute a kind of subtext; nevertheless, they themselves are not autobiographies.

An autobiography's controlling, retrospective point of view can be complicated in various ways. Mill and Spencer can work at their autobiographies at different points in their lives and careers; Ruskin can incorporate an autobiographical account written over a decade earlier for *Fors Clavigera* into the early chapters of *Praeterita*. The style of volume 1 may differ slightly from that of volume 2; or, in Ruskin's case, the early chapters may differ somewhat in style from the subsequent ones. Nevertheless, whether the writer was middle-aged and healthy or near death at the time of composition, he or she is identified with a unified persona, the autobiographer, who has begun to write the account of his or her life after reaching a certain stage of maturity and a certain aesthetic and moral distance from the time at which the narrative begins.

Many Victorian autobiographers choose to write *ex morte*, as if from beyond the grave. This device implies objectivity and detachment and strongly reinforces the retrospective quality of the narrative. On the other hand, Gosse writes at the age of fifty-seven, with no immediate fear or expectation of death, but since his narrative ends at early adulthood, he can establish a retrospective point of view, and at the same time claim a relatively reliable and accurate memory.[9]

The term *prose narrative* also requires discussion. That an autobiography must be written in *prose* is a problematical assumption. In terms of nineteenth-century English autobiography, there is one great stumbling block: William Wordsworth's *The Prelude*, which is commonly referred to as an autobiography and, except for the fact that it is a poem, seems to meet the criteria demanded by Lejeune's definition. Though I recognize *The Prelude* to be a borderline case, I believe that it is right to exclude poetry from our working definition. Lyric poems, even extraordinarily long ones, have their own set of conventions that allow for a use of language somewhat different from that found in nonfiction prose. I believe that this line of argument will become clearer as we continue to mark the generic distinctions implicit in our definition.

That an autobiography is a narrative may seem to be a rather obvious proposition, but as Linda Peterson has emphasized in her work on Victorian autobiography, the autobiographer often devotes more space to hermeneutics than to actual narration.[10] Passages that explore the meaning of one's life often are more substantial than those that describe incidents or "tell the story" of one's life. Despite this typical emphasis on interpretation rather than plot, however, Lejeune is surely correct in identifying the autobiography as primarily a narrative.

Any attempt to describe a substantial portion of a human life must result in narrative, because each life is essentially a matter of linear development through time. The growth and subsequent deterioration of the human body is only its most obvious, outer, aspect. The mind must develop through time as well, and both body and mind are enmeshed in history. An interpretive essay based on one or two moments of time or on one or two incidents in a life probably would not constitute an autobiography, although we cannot say that an autobiography must cover an "entire" life. Introducing the concept of narrative necessarily brings up the essential matter of closure, seemingly problematical here because one cannot literally report one's own death. The end point of the typical autobiography is of course something other than death. In discussing the narrative structure of the Victorian autobiographies throughout this book, I will show that the "something other" is surprisingly consistent. However, Lejeune might have amended his definition to read "an *extended*, retrospective prose narrative," in order to exclude explicitly mere sketches, essays, or summary statements. Perhaps the adjective *book length* would have been in order.

Returning to Lejeune's definition as it really is, we now come to the most controversial phrase: "written by a real person concerning his own existence." The theoretical argument that any text cannot really refer to anything real outside itself is a familiar one,[11] and compounding the theoretical problem is the simple fact that critics and scholars routinely blur (or simply ignore) the generic distinction between the autobiography and the autobiographical novel. It is not at all unusual to read Thomas Carlyle's *Sartor Resartus,* or even a bildungsroman such as Charles Dickens's *David Copperfield* as an autobiography. Some would go further and consider a less obviously autobiographical novel such as Nathaniel Hawthorne's *Scarlet Letter* in this way,[12] or even works as various as Paul Valéry's long poem *La Jeune Parque,*[13] and William Wordsworth's *Essays upon Epitaphs.*[14] To read a work of any literary genre as an expression of selfhood—or as another example of the impossibility of expressing selfhood—is a legitimate enterprise, and since literary genres are historically determined, readers are continually rereading literary works from the past against new conventions.

However, Lejeune's return to an apparent distinction between fiction and nonfiction is justified by his appeal to a reader-based aesthetics, and this distinction is, in my opinion, crucial to the peculiar powers, as well as the weaknesses, of the autobiography. Although he admits that the text itself cannot establish referentiality to a real person, "[in] printed texts, responsibility for all enunciation is assumed by a person who is in the habit of placing his *name* on the cover of the book, and on the flyleaf, above or below the title of the volume. The entire existence of the person we call the *author* is summed up by this name: the only mark in the text of an unquestionable world-beyond-the-text, referring to a real person, which requires that we thus attribute to him, in the final analysis, the responsibility for the production of the whole written text." The social and literary convention by which the reader accepts the name of the author as "a person whose existence is certified by vital statistics and is verifiable" is called by Lejeune the "autobiographical pact."[15] In spite of the "shaping" process that the autobiographer inevitably imposes on the material, recognition of the autobiographical pact subverts Burton Pike's widely accepted assumption that "all autobiography is essentially fiction."[16] The conventions as formulated by Lejeune imply that any verifiably inaccurate statements in the autobiography will be seen as flaws.

Any proper name is of course a metaphor, a metaphor that alienates the named person from the inexpressible mystery of personal identity and assimilates him or her into a system of language. The Victorian autobiographer may express a feeling that his or her identity has been somehow fated or predetermined outside language or any social system but typically acknowledges in effect the limitations of language and works within the system to adjust the meanings associated with his or her name. In order to do this the writer must use language under the constraints defined by the autobiographical pact.

Lejeune is wise to describe the author identified by the proper name given on the cover and the title page as the one who is "in the final analysis" held responsible for the text. Perhaps Harriet Mill *should* have been listed as coauthor of John Stuart Mill's autobiography, but she was not.[17] Unless we are historians of the publishing industry, we can never be quite sure that an editor or even a whole series of editors has not figured in the production of a published text, but the conventions of publication tell us that a real person, identified by name, is the author of the book. If we turn to the familiar example of *Sartor Resartus*, neither the Editor nor Diogenes Teufelsdröckh is identical to either the real and verifiable author Thomas Carlyle or the "implied author," however similar he may be in terms of philosophy or spiritual experience.[18] Teufelsdröckh nowhere appears as a pseudonym for Carlyle. Readers face a fictional narrative with expectations very different from those with which they face an autobiography, and, though narrative form itself does not effectively define genre, it is certainly related to it.

A merely cursory comparison makes it obvious that Victorian autobiographies are very different from Victorian novels, even those novels that are narrated in the first person. Victorian novelists—led by the prolific master Charles Dickens and (if one is willing to consider the mystery novel a serious genre) Wilkie Collins—created novels with long, complex plots, with multiple points of dramatic tension, deferral of expectations, and suspense; it can be generalized that Victorian readers accepted certain assumptions about the power of imaginative narrative to shape coherent meanings by the manipulation of an imagined character through an imagined sequence of events. By comparison, the autobiography is on the one hand controlled by biological and social history—genealogical record, birth, education, career, publication record, and so on—and on the other hand by a few key turning points, internal and external events that lead to the development of a more or less static "self" that can be identified with the author-narrator. The narrative in which the protagonist becomes the author-narrator tends to function as an exemplary tale for the life philosophy of the author-narrator, mediating between these inner and outer events, and this tendency is all the more powerful when the author-narrator is closely identified with a strong philosophical (or theological) position, as are, for example, Mill, Newman, Martineau, and Spencer.[19]

Not only do some conventions of the genre specific to the age deny the Victorian autobiographer the plot of romantic love and marriage, ubiquitous in novels of the time, but the author-narrator is constantly tempted by the otherwise permissive conventions of the genre to take a perhaps final opportunity to communicate all sorts of information to the world, information that is dear to his or her heart but that sometimes does little or nothing to develop the narrative of self-development. One of the common forms this gesture takes is usually very significant, not in developing the narrative but in helping to define its end point: I call it the Augustinian coda,[20] a final chapter or two, or a portion of a chapter, in which the author addresses the themes or issues with which he or she is most passionately concerned, a sort of philosophical essay and apologia.

Lejeune's definition of autobiography is finally based on the conventions of book publication rather than a philosophical concept of selfhood or of autobiographicality as expressed in art. However, some further theoretical implications of his model should be considered. In autobiography, unlike the novel, it is conventional to identify the narrator, the "I" of the text, with the historical author, with the "implied" author in the text, and with the protagonist. But an "I" can potentially consist of multiple voices, as in a dialogue with oneself, and the retrospective nature of the autobiographical narrative routinely leads to aesthetic distance between the narrator and the protagonist, who may even be referred to in the third person.[21] Again, for Lejeune, it is the proper name of the author as announced by the book, the "pledge of responsibility of a *real person*,"[22] that enables the stabilization and unification of the potentially diverse identities implied by the text.

If we consider the autobiography as a speech act or a performance, we imagine the writer attempting to stabilize and unify the

Introduction

text in this manner. He or she must show how the protagonist becomes the author-narrator. Newman's protagonist at the beginning is a Protestant, while Martineau's youthful protagonist is a Unitarian who writes religious tracts, and Gosse's is a young man "dedicated" to God by his parents and intended for the clergy. In each case, how did the protagonist develop into the author-narrator who is known to the public (represented by the implied reader) as a very different sort of person? That is the central problem to be worked out in the text.

The final stipulation of Lejeune's definition, that the focus of the autobiographer is on "his individual life, in particular the story of his personality," harkens back to Pascal's emphasis on the inner self rather than the outside world. Again, I believe that we should interpret our working definition as flexible enough to include sizable components of memoirs, reminiscences, and so forth, as long as the emphasis is on the individual self. For example, Mary Augusta Ward's *A Writer's Recollections* focuses on family members, associates, and current events to such an extent that its status as an autobiography must be seriously questioned.[23] However, what happens consistently in the autobiographies under consideration here—all of them by published authors—is that the selfhood or personality of the protagonist in the course of the narrative comes to be identified with the selfhood or personality of the author as expressed not only in the autobiography itself but in earlier published works as well. Typically, the publication of books provides many of the principal events of the plot, and it is the public, "published" persona incorporated into the mature works of the author rather than some hitherto secret or hidden personality that is explained and justified in the autobiography.[24]

To extend the notion of the social contract as expressed by Lejeune's "autobiographical pact," the Victorian autobiographer is expressly identified with a world beyond the text and with the public figure named on the title page, but in the case of previously published writers, the author is most closely identified with his or her other books, and they become the principal focus of the autobiographical text. The autobiography becomes a key to understanding and evaluating the author's published oeuvre. Published books exist in the "real world," as artifacts, as public documents, but through the conventions of reading they also present the author as a socially constructed persona. In the process of redefining or stabilizing that persona, the autobiographer is expected to conform to the "documented" facts of history. Victorian autobiographers are assumed to be sincere in everything they report, though they may legitimately conceal (and are expected to conceal) many of the details of their personal lives and any interior experience that is irrelevant to their place in society or, more specifically, irrelevant to previous publicly expressed ideas and res gestae or works—works usually corresponding to books.

Previous scholars have shown that many Victorian autobiographies, including some of those under consideration here, extend the generic conventions of the earlier English spiritual autobiography, especially by employing the strategy of biblical typology in the tradition of John Bunyan's *Grace Abounding to the Chief of Sinners* (1666).[25] I acknowledge the fact that displaced biblical imagery and narrative patterns can be found throughout Victorian autobiography, along with other archetypal forms that I will analyze in the individual works. However, when this spiritual tradition is defined as the dominant one, with scientific autobiographies seen as deviating from it to form a new model, a sense of continuity within a more embracing tradition is lost.

I am thinking of the "life and career" autobiography that perhaps finds its first full expression in Edward Gibbon's *Memoirs of My Life* (1796), which came to be popularly known as his Autobiography. (Even Newman, the great Victorian spiritual autobiographer, is primarily concerned with his public career and reputation.) Wayne Shumaker points out that Gibbon's was the first extended "secular" autobiography by a prominent Englishman to be printed and widely disseminated within a few years of his death and that it began to create "what had hitherto been lacking, a definite, competent, and inimitable tradition."[26] David Hume's *Life* (1777), which Gibbon cites as a modern English precedent to his own autobiography, consists of only a few pages. Should we take the 1796 publication date of Gibbon's *Memoirs* then as a defining moment in the historical development of the autobiography as it emerges—to borrow the terminology of Michael McKeon in his study of the English novel—as a "simple abstraction"?[27] Perhaps; in this view autobiography could be seen as attaining "'institutional' stability and coherence" at this time because of its power to explain the "selfhood" of a public personality, especially a published author.[28]

Gibbon's status as an historian writing his own history is suggestive. In his day, the historian was the most popular sort of writer—"History is the most popular species of writing, since it can adapt itself to the highest or the lowest capacity"[29]—and Gibbon identifies himself throughout his autobiography as preeminently a man of letters.[30] In the Victorian era, as well (to an extent difficult to imagine in this day of specialized and academic audiences), the scientists, philosophers, and other cultural sages shared with novelists the concept of a generalized public audience. Spencer was an engineer, inventor, and scientist, whose "literary career" led him to philosophy. Martineau first gained a wide audience with her popular series on political economy, and she was serious about the scientific basis of her works, but she always identified herself as primarily a *writer*, a producer of texts. Even Darwin foregrounds his concern with his works as *publications.*

There is a complicating factor, however. Gibbon himself did not really produce a unified text of the autobiography; instead, he left at his death six distinct autobiographical fragments, which were consolidated into a single narrative by his friend, Lord Sheffield. Not surprisingly, the Sheffield edition, which until recent times remained the only available one, omitted and distorted portions of Gibbon's original manuscripts.[31] We may appeal to Lejeune's model and point out that Edward Gibbon is identified as the author on the title page. However, the related issues of multiple authorship and intentionality impinge on the genre of autobiography in special ways that should be addressed here in order to anticipate problematic cases among the Victorian autobiographies to be discussed, especially Mill's. In autobiography, as already discussed, the author implied by the text[32] is conventionally identified with both the narrator in the text and the historical author named on the title page. The convention of adopting a unified, retrospective point of view, supposed to be that of the mature protagonist as well as that of the narrator, avoids the potential problem of various irreconcilable implicit selves in the text. And autobiographies, for obvious reasons, seldom go through multiple editions during the author's lifetime, so that the problem of choosing among variant published texts—so common in the novel—is rare. However, when there is evidence of substantial intervention by a collaborative author or editor in the text, fundamental problems of interpretation may be raised. If the "myth of the author as a single entity" has been nearly universally accepted until fairly recently in discussions of the novel,[33] the same has been true of autobiography, and, for this genre, the consequences of dissolving the myth may be even more striking. A "socialized concept of authorship and textual authority" like that of Jerome McGann may seem especially peculiar when applied to a story of oneself.[34]

And yet Lejeune's approach to autobiography has already led us to consider the historicity of text production as a fundamental aspect of the genre. If we always begin with the assumption that a real person wrote the narrative of which he or she is the center of interest, it is only natural that we explore the problematics of the verb *to write* (which sometimes can mean *to dictate*, among other things). Under what circumstances did the autobiographer write, and how was the manuscript or set of manuscripts translated into a printed book? A fictional protagonist's entire self can be imagined to be expressed in a novel, but the autobiography as nonfiction invites the reader to move continually from the text to the world beyond and back again. If the autobiographer, like Gibbon, leaves behind only a group of manuscript fragments, we cannot be sure that any one integrative plan matches his or her "true intentions," though we may have ample evidence by which to judge Bonnard's modern edition, let us say, superior to Lord Sheffield's. In other cases, like that of Mill, we accept the published version though we know it has been strongly influenced by a collaborator during the composition process and "tampered with" after the author's death.[35] And, according to the conventions of the genre, we may legitimately compare it to other more or less reliable historical sources for accuracy.

Despite its complicated origins, Gibbon's autobiography remained popular throughout the nineteenth century and clearly anticipates the genre as it is represented in the later works that we will discuss. Gibbon's res gestae, life-and-career mode not only accommodates Protestant biblical typology and other spiritual paradigms but also the Romantic "crisis pattern,"[36] various historical paradigms,[37] and of course "scientific" models of development such as that of biological evolution. By including both Newman and Mill, both Trollope and Darwin, both Ruskin and Spencer in my analyses, I hope to demonstrate continuities that justify the application of Lejeune's definition and the consideration of Victorian autobiographies as a nonfiction prose genre.

Chapter 1

John Henry Cardinal Newman, *Apologia pro Vita Sua* (1864)

Cardinal Newman's *Apologia* originally appeared in seven pamphlets, from 21 April to 2 June 1864. A book version, with the subtitle *Being a Reply to a Pamphlet Entitled "What, Then, Does Dr. Newman Mean?"* was published later in the same year. Newman made several revisions to the text prior to the 1886 edition, which is used in this study.

The *Apologia* is generally regarded as one of the masterpieces of Victorian nonfiction prose, and the controversy between Newman and the novelist Charles Kingsley that served as its occasion has been widely discussed. Briefly stated, in an unsigned December 1863 review of James Anthony Froude's *History of England* in *Macmillan's Magazine*, Kingsley commented that "Truth, for its own sake, had never been a virtue with the Roman clergy. Father Newman informs us that it need not, and on the whole ought not to be."[1] After Kingsley was identified as the writer, Newman challenged Kingsley to cite a source for this apparent justification of lying, but in the subsequent correspondence and exchange of pamphlets, Kingsley never did so, and in March 1864 wrote a fierce attack on Newman entitled *What, Then, Does Mr. Newman Mean?* Newman began to write the *Apologia* specifically as a reply to this pamphlet, apparently because he believed that all his present and future public works would be devalued unless he was able to save his reputation. As it turned out, he was strikingly successful: there can be little doubt that Newman's reputation rose, while Kingsley's sank, as a direct result of the publication of *Apologia pro Vita Sua*.

Newman's work has the most specific rhetorical purpose of any major Victorian autobiography, but it meets the requirements of our working definition of the genre. The *Apologia* can be profitably studied by the same methods that are applied to any other autobiography, for in answering Kingsley's charge that he has condoned the practice of lying, Newman offers the story of his life as proof of personal integrity. Though he considers only one part of his life, the history of his religious opinions, it is at the heart of his total interpretation of his life, both as an individual and as a public figure. In drawing out the history of his mind, Newman will "give the true key to my whole life" (11–12).

It is a commonplace that St. Augustine's *Confessions* is the first real autobiography, and in a broad sense, all the forms of autobiography can be traced back to that fifth-century classic. In the case of Newman's *Apologia*, however, the special relevance of the *Confessions* is obvious. Newman's work is eminently a spiritual autobiography, by far the most significant Victorian example and a Catholic one at that.

Newman was undoubtedly conscious of Augustine when he wrote the *Apologia*, but he was aware of the Protestant tradition of spiritual autobiographies as well. Linda Peterson has shown how Newman adapted both English Protestant and Augustinian narrative forms in constructing his own story.[2]

Thomas Scott's *Force of Truth* (1779) had been an important early influence in Newman's spiritual development, as he himself reports (17). When he came to write the *Apologia* he located in Scott's autobiography a model of development quite different from the essentially irrational, highly emotional one found in John Bunyan's *Grace Abounding* (1666) and in many other evangelical works. Unlike Bunyan, Scott traced a highly rational process of personal religious growth and change generated by a continual study of biblical and ecclesiastical sources. When Newman tells the "history of his religion opinions," particularly in his first two chapters, he is using a very similar method, except that he pays little attention to biblical references and instead concentrates on Church history and tradition. The lack of biblical allusions not only follows from his Catholic theological stance but also from his avoidance of the biblical typology characteristic of Protestant spiritual autobiographies, especially the Exodus imagery of a journey from "wilderness" to "promised land." Newman shifts into the Catholic Augustinian narrative pattern in his fourth chapter, as he introduces the metaphors of sickness, death, and resurrection to describe his break with the Anglican Church and conversion to Catholicism.[3] At that point the narrative in effect ends, and his final chapter of personal reflection on his belief is a *confessio fidei* parallel to Augustine's personal and theological reflections in his final four books.

Recognition of the Scott and Augustine models aids our understanding of the *Apologia*, but certain differences between Newman and Augustine are crucial to understanding the nineteenth-century work. Aside from the considerably different rhetorical stance, the narrative structure of the *Apologia* is somewhat different.

Although Augustine as narrator points out signs that the unconverted protagonist's destiny, through God's will, is to join the Church, he is not concerned with analyzing a process or development of mind. Before his conversion he was one thing; then he became another. The point of conversion marks an absolute change in his life. Newman's conversion to Catholicism, the analogous climactic event in his life story, is not really equivalent to Augustine's conversion. Newman was converted to Christianity in 1816 at the age of fifteen. From that time, "impressions of dogma . . . have never been effaced or obscured" (16). Newman tells the reader almost nothing about his life prior to that conversion. He is absolutely committed to Christianity at the beginning of his narrative. The only question for him is what duties and affiliations his identity as a Christian entails. The essential meaning of his life is held by his account of the development, one could say the evolution, of his mind, that led him to those proper duties and affiliations. However, once he has found them, in the Catholic Church, his search is over. Further development is out of the question: "From the time that I became a Catholic [in 1845], of course I have no further history of my religious opinions to narrate. . . . I have had no variations to record, and have had no anxiety of heart whatever. I have been in perfect peace and contentment; I never have had one doubt" (184). Thus Newman's development of mind is a development or evolution within absolute boundaries.

Aside from the implications of Newman's Protestant and Catholic narrative models, it is useful to consider the narrative form of the *Apologia*, without reference to literary history.

By strictly limiting his material, Newman gives his life story a particularly strong focus. Throughout his five chapters, the plot is clearly defined by the movement of his mind, that is, change of opinion in religious matters. Thus each move or change of opinion becomes a function in the plot.[4] However, this seemingly straightforward syntagmatic structure is complicated, as in the case of many autobiographies, by the fact that mental, interior events or changes have external consequences that do not necessarily correspond to them in time or emphasis. Newman minimizes this problem by carefully coordinating mental events with his own actions and with the social consequences of these actions. Most significantly, virtually all foregrounded mental events are closely linked to contemporary literary acts—passages from books, essays, or letters. Generally, these events are thus documented in proportion to their relative significance; Newman's literary acts then are linked to his developing position in society, especially as regards the course of the Tractarian movement. Furthermore, his chapter divisions signify a carefully delineated, larger narrative structure.

In chapter 1, "History of My Religious Opinions to the Year 1833," Newman passes quickly over his preconversion, "superstitious" self, that is, prior to age fifteen in 1816, but his description of his old habit of crossing himself when going into the dark and the apparent sketch of a rosary in an old copybook prefigure his later life and imply a sense of destiny. After briefly describing his conversion, which was inspired by the Calvinistic books lent him by the Rev. Walter Meyers, his evangelist mentor at Ealing, Newman traces one religious influence after another: the autobiography and other writings of Scott, which helped to turn him away from the errors of Calvinism; the writings of Joseph Milnes and Thomas Newton in church history; the early Oxford influence of Oriel fellows Richard Whately and Edward Hawkins (who later were to oppose Newman and the Tractarians); Bishop Joseph Butler's *Analogy*; the portentous meetings with John Keble, and later with Keble's pupil Hurrell Froude; the writings of the church fathers; his voyage abroad with Hurrell Froude and his father, during which his antiliberal opinions accelerated; and his return home in July 1833, to see the Oxford movement effectively begun by Keble's "Assize Sermon." Each book and each individual is associated with a turn in religious thought, though Newman cannot be precise in outlining this course in these early, largely "undocumented" years. For example, after discussing his chronological reading of the church fathers, he writes, "I do not know when I first learned to consider that Antiquity was the true exponent of the doctrines of Christianity and the basis of the Church of England; but I take it for granted that the works of Bishop Bull, which at this time I read, were my chief introduction to this principle" (33). Even in this first chapter, however, Newman studies his own essays in attempting to trace the evolution of his ideas concerning miracles (30).

Beginning with chapter 2, "History of My Religious Opinions from 1833 to 1839," Newman's self-history becomes linked to the history of the Oxford, or Tractarian, movement and becomes from this point increasingly a history of his publications, with incremental use of documentation—references and quotations from his published works and private letters that illustrate his ideas at a particular time. Although he gives a detailed summary of his religious position in these years—with its three fundamental points of dogma, the visible Church with its sacraments and rites as channels of grace, and anti-Romanism—he continues to acknowledge the limits of memory. For example he "cannot tell" when he finally gave up the notion of the pope as Antichrist (53).

The principal plot functions are the publication of Newman's writings: the tracts that marked his active role in the movement; a book entitled *Prophetical Office of the Church*, which developed the doctrine of an Anglican Via Media between Protestantism and Roman Catholicism; an "Essay on Justification," against the Lutheran doctrine of justification by faith only; a pamphlet entitled *The Church of the Fathers*. Newman's treatment of the one important plot function in this chapter that does not involve his writings illustrates an underlying structural problem. After describing the entry of the influential Edward B. Pusey into the movement, Newman inserts the following metadiscourse:

> But I must return to myself. I am not writing the history of either Dr. Pusey or of the Movement; but it is a pleasure to me to have been able to introduce here reminiscences of the place which we held in it, which have so direct a bearing upon myself, that they are no digression from my narrative. (61)

This passage brings to the surface Newman's impulse to integrate a larger story of historical development into his self-history and the tension between this impulse and his desire to present his own story in the most economical and dramatic form.

Chapter 3, "History of My Religious Opinions from 1839 to

1841," appropriately covers the shortest span of historical time because it details the central crisis or turning point in Newman's story. Although he begins the chapter by announcing that he is about to trace "as far as I can the course of that great revolution of mind, which led me to leave my own home" and calls this task the boldest thing he has ever done in his life (81), the narrative moves slowly. Exercising ever greater care and precision in tracing his mental development, Newman appears to alter his technique of closely coordinating inner and outer plot functions by devoting over half of his chapter to his "state of mind" during the period 1839–41, before turning to "how my new misgivings affected my conduct, and my relations towards the Anglican Church" (106).

The narrative continuity of the first two chapters is blurred, then, and the text becomes much more discursive. Two major events occur in this chapter: the interior one in the summer of 1839 when "for the first time a doubt came upon me of the tenableness of Anglicanism" (96) and the publication of the controversial Tract 90 in February of 1841. The inner event is more prominently foregrounded and is carefully prepared for.

A summary of Newman's article on "The State of Religious Parties" from the spring of 1839 (81–89) is followed by what he terms a "dry discussion" of the controversy between the Anglican Church and Rome (89–92) that focuses on the central issue of antiquity versus Catholicity, followed by extracts from writings of 1836, 1840, and 1841 to illustrate "the status of the controversy" (92–96). Now the narrative as such resumes. In studying the history of the Monophysites during the summer of 1839, Newman was struck by the parallel between the fifteenth-century, heretical sect and Protestants of his own day. Newman quotes his own later account of the revelation: "It was difficult to make out how the Eutychians or Monophysites were heretics, unless Protestants and Anglicans were heretics also" (97).

Tract 90, with its thesis that the Thirty-nine Articles had been written with an intentional ambiguity and that, properly read, they did not conflict with Roman Catholic doctrine, marked the end of Newman's acceptability to the Anglican bishops. Two other interior events coincided with his realization that he was no longer acceptable: a historical study of the Arian heresy reinforced his idea that all

Protestants were in schism with the Church, and Anglican plans for a Jerusalem bishopric, which amounted to "courting an intercommunion with Protestant Prussians and the heresy of the Orientals," appalled him.

Chapter 4, "History of My Religious Opinions from 1841 to 1845," begins with Newman's statement that he was on his "deathbed" regarding his membership in the Anglican Church from the end of 1841. "A death-bed has scarcely a history; it is a tedious decline, with seasons of rallying and seasons of falling back; and since the end is foreseen . . . it has little interest for the reader" (121). In spite of Newman's metaphor, however, this final narrative chapter tells a story of acceptance as well as rejection.

As Newman became increasingly uneasy in his Anglican role (even as a layman) and severed his ties with the church one by one, he removed the obstacles that had heretofore prevented him from seriously considering conversion to Catholicism. Once again, the chapter is largely composed of extracts from letters that explain his state of mind at a particular time. Newman reemphasizes his need to document his story in this way, "as I cannot rely on my memory" (121). The plot functions involving outer actions in this chapter are his formal retraction of his former criticism of the Catholic Church, his resignation of the living of St. Mary's, his conversion to the Catholic Church, and his final, physical leaving of Oxford. The story of the movement also is carried forward by a significant event: the appearance of a faction of eager young activist followers who had had no part in the early days of the movement and the doctrine of the via media.

Though Newman's sympathy for Rome was gradually expanding, the one remaining necessary step was to convince himself by reason that he could accept the Catholic Church with certitude. He was able to take this last intellectual step after working hard on his *Essay on the Development of Christian Doctrine* throughout most of 1845. The essay remained unfinished, but "[b]efore I got to the end, I resolved to be received" (181). This intellectual exercise lifted the final obstacle to Newman's acceptance because he was now able to account for the accretion of doctrine in the Church since antiquity. The Anglican claim to antiquity as opposed to Catholicity was now definitively answered: "I saw that the principle of development not only accounted for certain facts, but was in itself a remarkable philosophical phenomenon... discernible from the first years of the Catholic teaching up to the present day" (156).

In chapter 5, "Position of My Mind since 1845," Newman immediately announces the end of the narrative portion of his autobiography; there will be no further history to relate. His mind remained active but development was brought to an abrupt end.

Critics have called attention to the dramatic narrative structure of the *Apologia*, with its crisis in chapter 3 and resolution in chapter 4, and have compared it to the classical epic structure (a comparison encouraged by Newman's allusions to Virgil and Homer).[5] One of the most revealing approaches to the *Apologia*'s narrative structure, however, has been to compare it to the archetypal process of mental development that Newman outlines in his other works, most comprehensively in *Grammar of Assent* (1870). For example, in adopting Newman's own language in his presentation of the embryo theory in the *Apologia* itself, Robert A. Colby shows how Newman in his extremely complex development progresses through the stages of denunciation and rejection (of Catholicism); toleration; doubt, suspicion, and surmise; belief; and certitude.[6] Frequently quoted phrases from this part of the *Apologia* reinforce this idea: "I had a great dislike of paper logic.... It is the concrete being that reasons... the whole man moves" (136).

The structural models of spiritual autobiography by Augustine and Scott that inform the *Apologia* have already been alluded to. As other nineteenth-century British autobiographies are examined in later chapters, it will become clear that Newman's work also has much in common with the Romantic crisis pattern, most clearly illustrated in Carlyle's fictional *Sartor Resartus*, and with Mill's autobiography. Despite his much-protested reliance on reason rather than emotion, Newman does report the typical confusion, stress, and anguish that accompanies the archetypal crisis of personality leading to a new identity, commitment, and life goal.

On a higher level of abstraction, however, Newman may be said to describe a process of change or development that ends in stasis. If, adapting Colby's scheme, we take the structure of rejection—toleration—surmise—belief—certitude as a series of plot functions, we have a syntagm that potentially could be applied to any significant change of belief or commitment over time. But it is more than that for

Newman. Because he defines his selfhood in terms of religious commitment, the story (history of his mind) is "the key to my whole life." Furthermore, this underlying narrative structure is significant in a larger sense because it corresponds to his model of historical change. The mechanism Newman outlined in the crucial *Essay on the Development of Christian Doctrine* that allowed him to accept the apparent Catholic "additions" to Primitive Church doctrine is the gradual historical explication and interpretation of the revelation of external truth (entire in itself), that had in fact been provided by God at the beginning of the Christian era. In the final chapter of the *Apologia*, Newman describes the slow, painstaking process whereby the Church establishes a "new" doctrine (the Immaculate Conception, for example) that is finally felt and understood to be completely in harmony with previously established dogma. As in the case of the individual, who, through an agonizingly slow, complex psychological and philosophical process, arrives at certitude, the community of Christians finally accepts the doctrine that has been true all along. Thus, as Newman struggles toward the end point of his own personal development, he also plays a part in the larger historical evolution toward divine truth. The flux of social life that surrounds him—ferment in the institutional life of university, church, nation—is part of this universal, historical process.

It is in the context of this all-encompassing narrative that we see Newman's peculiar genius for describing with great delicacy the emotional and irrational or intuitive psychological states that necessarily accompany rational thought in matters of personal belief and commitment. That is, Newman's self-presentation, his intimate portrayal of intricate human experience, is enclosed in a larger pattern of meaning. The fear of the constant chaotic flux of human experience, of being cut off from the past and the resultant disintegration of the individual personality; the yearning for overarching patterns of meaning and the sometimes desperate search for certainties—these widely discussed nineteenth- and twentieth-century literary and cultural themes help to explain the unique appeal and also the ambiguous status of Newman's autobiography. It presents a version of deeply felt, universal humanism enclosed within a coherent historical and religious context and invites the reader to share this experience on a personal, "Romanticized" level: on the one hand shared experience in the Romantic tradition, on the other hand protection from the potential endless variety of experience in personal submission to dogma.

Of course, aside from his universal vision, Newman was consciously speaking to an audience of the English public composed of specific subgroups, among them his old Oxford associates who had remained Anglican, and his fellow English Catholics. His rhetorical devices have been analyzed by a number of scholars.[7] I will approach some of these rhetorical considerations here in the process of examining paradigmatic oppositions in Newman's autobiography.

As with all autobiography, Newman the narrator is cut off from himself as the protagonist of his story by a greater or lesser gap of memory-effacing time. At the critical point of his conversion to Catholicism, the gap is about twenty years between the time of the story and the present time of the text, and the earliest references in the book are to a childhood over fifty years distant. At the beginning of chapter 3, the narrator acknowledges the enormity of the task before him, as he confronts the darkness and confusion of the past. In the final chapter, however, protagonist and narrator are merged into a single self in the text's present time.

There is no extreme disjunction between the preconversion protagonist and the narrator as in the archetypal conversion story, Augustine's *Confessions*. After all, Newman as implied author seeks to persuade the reader that there is in fact a well-defined continuity between the Anglican and Catholic Newmans, an unbroken sense of honesty and integrity, as the young man inevitably becomes the narrator Newman. Of course, the reader gets a very brief glimpse of the pagan child before his life-altering conversion to Christianity and sees that the young man flirted with Calvinism and then with Liberalism before entering into his Anglo-Catholic stage, the stage with which the narrative proper begins. Even then, the author-narrator employs a mild distancing irony throughout most of the story. For example, in his early activity for the movement, "my behavior had a mixture in it both of fierceness and sport; and on this account, I dare say, it gave offense to many; nor am I here defending it" (48). In a limited sense Newman makes use of the Romantic confessional mode associated with Rousseau. In Newman's case, the narrator "tells all," as far as memory and available documents will allow, and within the restricted scope of the narrative, since private experience itself is the primary evidence in support of the book's argument, that is, for Newman's integrity.

Because of the delicate balance between change and continuity in the context of a "cultural debate," the relationship between narrator and protagonist in this autobiography is precarious, and Newman has been widely admired for his success in negotiating it.

Past time is not readily accessible through memory in the present time of the book, and the narrator relies largely on quotation from letters and essays to sustain his narrative of development. Past events are reconstructed, much as in the preparation of a legal case. However, a sense of inevitability, in spite of the complexity of experience, implies a continuity that makes the essential meaning of the past retrievable. A sense of its inevitability is achieved by a sharply focused plot, which associates certain vivid memories with strong impressions, at key points, and by allusions to omens and intuitions. The book implies that present time is really the past two decades, that is, the time since Newman's conversion to Catholicism in 1845. Memory need not be troubled past that point because a permanent sense of selfhood has been achieved. Newman's claim to stasis after 1845 may strike some readers as disingenuous, but his metaphor of coming into a port after a rough journey at sea (184) is perfectly suited to the cessation of narrative time.

In tension with the implacable forward movement in narrative form, however, there is a strong sense of nostalgia in the *Apologia*, especially that associated with memories of university life at Oxford. Newman's understated description of leaving Oxford for the last time, with its snapdragon, his private symbol for "perpetual residence even unto death in my University" (183), is appropriate to a Victorian literary tradition replete with powerful images of lost, Edenic time and place. The *Apologia* is in a sense a story of severance from home and family, for the largely self-contained world of Oxford and its university men occupy the place of home and family found in some other autobiographies. The new home and family in the Church is outside the time of the narrative and not described in concrete detail in the discursive final chapter.

In addition to the nostalgia for Oxford as a physical place, the *Apologia* also conveys a strong sense of the university as a hierarchical institution, heavy with symbolic value. The protagonist must break away from his beloved home to follow his vision of truth, but the retrospective author-narrator affectionately reminisces about old Oxford friends and associates.

Even more complex than the narrator-protagonist relationship is that between Newman as narrator and his implied audience. As several critics have pointed out, Newman's potential antagonists are not limited to Liberals, Evangelists, and Broad Church Anglicans who sympathize with Charles Kingsley's point of view; they also include former friends in the English church who feel betrayed and even fellow Catholics who have grown suspicious of him.

In his preface, Newman carefully defines and appeals to his audience, the English public. He assumes that he will be able to break through the barrier of prejudice that surrounds him because Englishmen, his countrymen, will be generous and repentant for their past injustice (8). He both flatters and chastises his English audiences, in the best Victorian sage tradition. His rhetorical position is perhaps more difficult than any ever assumed by Carlyle, Ruskin, or Arnold, however much they may have shifted their views through the years: Newman had once spoken to the public, not only as an Anglican, but an anti-Catholic. It is the tension between Newman and his public audience rather than the tension between Newman and God that provides most of the drama in this "true story" of a man who changed his mind: this in itself sets the *Apologia* apart from most of the earlier English spiritual autobiographies. In his classic study of the *Apologia* Walter Houghton offered a perceptive analysis of Newman's rhetorical strategies. Newman's confession of personal faults and errors and his recognition of the difficulties of faith "could not but make him peculiarly sympathetic to the British public of the 1860s."[8] Also significant are his "marked strain of modesty" (especially in playing down his leadership in the Oxford movement), "the impression of unselfish warmth and generosity" (even for men like Edward Hawkins and Richard Whately, with whom he was known to have quarreled), and his self-portrait as an "innocent and pathetic victim of persecution."[9]

Newman's claim that he is only giving the true history of his mind and not writing "controversially" allows him to assert his opposition to the principle of Liberalism as a strongly felt personal belief throughout his autobiography while deemphasizing or ignoring arguments with specific opponents. In terms of references to individuals, the narrative becomes not only a recreation of bygone days but also an imaginative renewal of old friendships and reconciliation of old misunderstandings. On the other hand, Newman accepts his role as defender of his Catholic brethren against unfair charges of dishonesty and duplicity and ends by emphasizing his ties to the Church in his final chapter, notably in his dedication of his self-history, "as a memorial of affection and gratitude" (215) to the priests of the Birmingham Oratory, which Newman founded and where he served as superior. Whether or not one wants to read this memorial and the following references to Ambrose St. John on the model of Augustine's elegy for his mother Monica, as a substitution for the mother with whom he had broken over his conversion to Rome, the communal sense is obvious. The profoundly fraternal tone of the book is linked to its narrative structure—as the protagonist gravitates toward the true community of mankind, the narrator appeals to the commonality of human experience and the universal need for a common ground that supersedes the anarchical private response to life.

Paradoxically one man's experience is offered up as an implied argument for the transcendence of private experience. The protagonist rejects by degrees the static (Anglican) argument of antiquity and accepts by degrees the developmental argument of Catholicity. By the end of the narrative, the problem of time has been solved, on the philosophical and theological level as well as on the level of individual experience. In this way, Newman has moved well beyond the factional disputes and concerns associated with specific audiences to a universal level that allows his autobiography to be read as a genuinely prophetic book.[10] Finally, Newman's apologia—so specific and topical in its references to dates and documents—is defense, explanation, and justification, in the broadest sense of these terms.

Chapter 2

John Stuart Mill, *Autobiography* (1873)

John Stuart Mill wrote the first draft of his *Autobiography* before Newman wrote the *Apologia*, in the period 1853–54, when he was only forty-seven. Apparently at this time he thought that both he and his wife Harriet were dying of tuberculosis. Following the death of his wife in 1858, Mill revised and extended the 1853–54 text in 1861 and then completed the final version of the manuscript by "bringing it up to date" in the winter of 1869–70. The *Autobiography* was not published until the year of his death, 1873, in a posthumous edition. Mill's text probably has been analyzed in print even more extensively than Newman's. Not only is the book of considerable interest for the reasons Mill himself believed—because it is a well-written portrait of an intellectual's mental development during a great age of transition—but also because it raises fascinating psychological and textual questions that Mill no doubt would not have appreciated. What were the full dimensions of his relationship with the remarkable, domineering father who taught him Greek by the age of three? What were the underlying (unconscious) causes of his "mental crisis" and of his idolization of his wife Harriet Mill (the former Harriet Taylor)? To what extent did Harriet Mill collaborate with Mill in writing the text? These questions have been discussed widely, and the last one is particularly provocative in its implications for the genre. According to the conventions of autobiography as we have defined them, Mill and no one else is the author of his autobiography, although, in the process of relating the text to the historical Mill, the reader naturally takes into account what he knows about the problematics of text production.[1]

Unlike the *Apologia*, Mill's *Autobiography* incorporates features of the full-scale res gestae treatment of the life and career of a public figure of which Edward Gibbon's *Memoirs*, discussed in chapter 1, is an early example. Mill at least begins his self-history with childhood and treats his father as a major character in his story, even if he does almost completely ignore his mother and his siblings. Like Newman, however, Mill has given the plot of his narrative a sharp focus by concentrating on his mental history, or the history of his opinions, and he gives three specific reasons for writing his autobiography. One is to provide a record of his "unusual and remarkable" education, which "has proved how much more than is commonly supposed may be taught, and well taught, in those early years which, in the common modes of what is called instruction, are little better than wasted." Another reason is that "in an age of transition in opinions, there may be somewhat both of interest and of benefit in noting the successive phases of any mind which was always pressing forward." And most importantly to Mill, his autobiography will acknowledge "the debts which my intellectual and moral development owes to other persons," in particular, "the one to whom most of all is due, one whom the world had no opportunity of knowing" (3), that is, his wife Harriet. Once again, then, private, inner experience will be used as evidence in asserting public truth and correcting the historical record.

The "successive phases of mind" signify much more than a history of Mill's opinions in a narrow sense. Mill is the quintessential man of ideas. His developing philosophy of life is as central to his self-concept as religion is to Newman's. All personal aspects of his life, including his "profession" as an official at the East India Company, are subordinated to his work as a philosopher and writer. His friends and associates, including the two dominant personalities in his life, are described in terms of their relation to his ideas, the father almost to the exclusion of familial love, his longtime friend and wife to the exclusion of sexual love.

Mill's first two chapters cover approximately the first fourteen years of his life (1806–20). In the first chapter he traces "Childhood and Early Education" up to 1820; in the second, he describes "Moral Influences in Early Youth" during that same period of time. Each chapter ends with the event that marked the end of Mill's education at home: his residence of about one year in France with the family of Sir Samuel Bentham.

Both chapters are dominated by Mill's relationship with his father. The first focuses on the father's system of education. Although it is largely comprised of descriptions of his father's stringent methods and reading lists, there is some narrative movement associated with educational stages: Greek and arithmetic prior to age eight; then Latin classics, along with private reading, followed by logic from about age twelve. The second chapter, which for the most part covers the same time period, is largely a description of his father's atheism and system of morality, along with his own first exposure to Jeremy Bentham and the Benthamites. However, at the end of the chapter, Mill includes a short description of his European stay that advances the narrative by referring to the deep impression made upon him by mountain scenes and to his introduction to "Continental Liberalism" in the society he met. These two events are the early stages of a movement away from the father's sphere of influence in symbolic as well as spatial terms: European liberalism implies a greater flexibility of thought, and the mountain scenery implies a Romantic, emotional response to experience that foreshadows his later study of Wordsworth.

The transitional chapter 3, "Last Stage of Education, and First of Self-Education," records Mill's development of a "unified, coherent philosophy," chiefly through his independent study of Bentham's works. Bentham's "principle of utility" became "[t]he keystone which held together the detached and fragmentary component parts of my knowledge and beliefs" (42). And although he continued to study analytic psychology under the direction of his father and was influenced by his father's friends, he wrote his first argumentative essay on his own initiative and founded the Utilitarian Society in 1823. His father obtained an appointment for him at the East India Company that was ideal for an independent thinker and writer, a position that he was to hold for the next thirty-five years.

Chapter 4, "Youthful Propagandism," carries the story forward about three years, though it contains references to some later events. Here at first Mill's story is once again closely linked to that of his father. He served as his father's understudy in a Radical political and cultural movement that gained momentum through the new *Westminster Review* and he acquired valuable experience in writing and publishing letters and articles. An important internal event is his disagreement with his father's lack of support for women's suffrage, but in general he and other young men under the influence of the elder Mill seized upon his ideas "with youthful fanaticism" (66).

However, toward the end of this period, the young protagonist begins to deemphasize sectarianism and ceases to refer to his group as "utilitarians." He markedly improves his writing style by editing some of Bentham's works and then begins to write essays that "were no longer mere reproductions and applications of the doctrines I had been taught; they were original thinking" (72). His participation in a discussion group with a few of his associates leads to his "own real inauguration as an original and independent thinker" (74), and afterward he takes an active part in a new Debating Society that occupies much of his intellectual energy.

Chapter 5 is perhaps the best-known chapter in Victorian autobiography: "A Crisis in My Mental History." Although it is largely discursive and hermeneutic, due to Mill's detailed cause-and-effect analysis of his mental changes, it presents the "mental crisis" as a single event in "the melancholy winter of 1826–27," a significant turning point of his life that led to years of transition in thought and feeling, and that, in retrospect, prepared him for the later influence of Harriet Taylor, whom he met in 1830. In a famous passage, Mill awakes "as from a dream" to ask himself whether he would be happy if all his "objects in life" were realized and all the "changes in institutions and opinions" that he supported were accomplished. "And an irrepressible self-consciousness distinctly answered, 'No!' At this my heart sank within me: the whole foundation on which my life was constructed fell down" (81). The incident that allowed Mill to begin to overcome his "hopeless" state was his spontaneous emotional response to a passage in Marmontel's *Memoirs* that describes Marmontel's resolution as a boy to take the place of his dead father as head of his family. "From this moment, my burden grew lighter" (85). Mill describes two major subsequent changes in his "opinions and character": his new theory that happiness can only be an indirect result of purposeful work rather than an end in itself and his new interest in the inner life of the individual and adoption of "the cultivation of the feelings" as "one of the cardinal points in my ethical and philosophical creed" (85–86). In following this new direction, he found "inward joy" in the poetry of Wordsworth and went on to develop new ways of thinking that further separated him from his father's rigid ideas concerning logic and political philosophy. Particularly influential on his evolving thought were the ideas of the Saint-Simonians and then of Comte, ideas that provided models for the "natural order of human progress" (98). On a more personal level, he was able to reconcile the troubling opposition of determinism and free will by concluding that "though our character is formed by circumstances, our own desires can do much to shape these circumstances" (102). He wrote prolifically on logic and political economy.

Chapter 6 records the "Commencement of the Most Valuable Friendship of My Life" (that is, with Harriet Taylor) and refers to his writings up to the year 1840 and to his father's death. In this final "stage" of mental progress, the central events are the substitution of Harriet Taylor for his father as the center of power and influence in Mill's life and then the gradual merging of his mental progress with hers in "complete companionship" (113). However, though Mill dwells on his "almost infinite" intellectual debt to her, he admits that by the time he met her "the only actual revolution which has ever taken place in my modes of thinking, was already complete" (114). The only "substantial changes of opinion" related to a qualified acceptance of socialism and modification of his political ideal of pure democracy (115). In this chapter, he notes his disagreements with Comte, continues his history of publications—most notably new work on his *Logic* and the well-known essays on Bentham and Coleridge—gives a very high assessment of his father's importance as leader of the intellectual radicals in England, and traces the fortunes of radical politics in the 1830s.

The concluding chapter 7, "General View of the Remainder of My Life," functions somewhat like the Augustinian coda to Newman's autobiography:

> From this time, what is worth relating of my life will come into a very small compass; for I have no further mental changes to tell of, but only, as I hope, a continued mental progress; which does not admit of a consecutive history, and the results of which, if real, will be found in my writings. I shall therefore greatly abridge the chronicle of my subsequent years. (132)

This first paragraph of the chapter is curious in that it effectively calls a halt to the narrative of Mill's mental life yet reports a continued "mental progress." As the passage suggests, Mill's mental life now becomes almost synonymous with his publications, and much of the chapter could be described as a sort of annotated bibliography. Ironically, despite Mill's claim to brevity now that the drama of development no longer controls the narrative, this loosely organized chapter becomes the longest in the book, although it proceeds in roughly chronological order up to the end of his service—and immersion in public issues—as MP for Westminster in 1868. He refers to his marriage with Harriet Taylor in 1851 and her death seven years later as "the most important events of my private life" (143) and makes claims for her influence, even joint authorship in his works, principally by her contribution of "the human element" (149) in "this third period (as it may be termed) of my mental progress" (137). The concluding description of his quiet life in southern Europe and continuing work for women's rights with his stepdaughter Helen Taylor is replete with reminders of his deceased wife. (She had died in Avignon.) Earlier he had stated that "her memory is to me a religion" (145). Thus, in a sense, Mill concludes, as does Newman, in a state of religious stasis.

Although Mill as author-narrator seems to be remarkably naive and unaware in describing himself and his motivations in relation to other individuals, he seems to be quite conscious of presenting a distinctive narrative of his self-development. As his introductory paragraph makes clear, he sees himself as a man in transition in an age of transition, and although he never became a disciple of the Saint-Simonians nor of Comte, he learned from them "the peculiarities of an era of transition" (100). Saint-Simon conceived of three "organic" periods of history, each unified by a philosophy or religion, divided by transitional, "critical" periods characterized by fragmentation. The first organic period, the Polytheistic, was followed by the Theological. In the 1830s, the world was in a critical period that would eventually lead to a new Positive era, a kind of golden age of science that would conclude the dynamic process of change.

As the narrator Mill sees it, he himself as protagonist was to progress through three definable stages of development. The first stage, "his youth and early education," under the dominating influence and strict guidance of his father, was itself characterized by a simple narrative of history, that is, the continuing progress of mankind through the application of rational thought. Although his father had introduced him to Benthamite ideas, Mill had never read Bentham for himself until the winter of 1821–22 (in the French rendition by Dumont), following his liberating year on the Continent. This was "one of the turning points in my mental history" (41) and apparently involved the transition into the second stage of "self-education," which would last only about five or six years, leading into the more traumatic transitional period of the mental crisis. However, the *Autobiography* implies that Mill, unlike his era, gradually moved into a mature stage of development analogous to the prophesied Positive stage of history (under the tutelage of Harriet Taylor).

Mill also implies that his self-history has affinities with evangelical Christian conversion narratives. His state of mind accompanying his mental crisis is "the state, I should think, in which converts to Methodism usually are, when smitten by their first 'conviction of sin'" (81). The irony here is considerable, since the postcrisis Mill isn't about to lose his status as an inveterate atheist.

Of course, he also says that his depressed mental state was exactly like that described in Coleridge's poem "Dejection: An Ode," compares the theory he adopted in reaction to his crisis to Carlyle's "anti-self-consciousness" theory from "Characteristics" and *Sartor Resartus*, and describes his subsequent readings of Wordsworth's poetry designed to "cultivate" his feelings. Extending the implication of these Romantic allusions in Mill, Jack Stillinger finds "striking parallels" between the development of Mill in his *Autobiography* and that of Wordsworth in *The Prelude*.[2]

The Romantic crisis pattern, as a narrative model, can be applied easily to Mill's *Autobiography*. The Romantic conception of an individual's life is based on the following process: the "self," which John N. Morris suggests is the modern equivalent for the traditional concept of "soul,"[3] typically undergoes an extreme and private experience, usually concerned with some kind of negation of personal values and accompanied by mental anguish, followed by a period of readjustment, and, finally, a higher level of understanding and a new commitment. The Romantic discovers in his own feelings and his own will a source of value in an otherwise meaningless universe. Then he attempts to achieve a positive formulation and to construct an external world in which he can believe. Robert Langbaum writes, "It makes no difference whether the romanticist arrives in the end at a new formulation or returns to an old one. It is the process of denial and reaffirmation which distinguishes him both from those who have never denied and those who, having denied, have never reaffirmed."[4] A description of this process forms the core of the Romantic's autobiography.

Each successive mental state can be described as a plot function in this syntagmatic narrative structure. Thus the "mental crisis" syntagm can be seen as an insert within the larger syntagm of plot functions associated with Mill's phased mental development.

Mill as narrator gives remarkably few descriptive details of physical environment, but he keeps the mind of his protagonist in sharp focus. Except at its farthest reaches, his memory seems exceptionally clear. "I have no remembrance of the time when I began to learn Greek. I have been told that it was when I was three years old. My earliest recollection on the subject, is that of committing to memory . . . lists of common Greek words (5). He faintly remembers "reading his first Greek book, Aesop's Fables." But once he reaches the point at which he had begun the study of Latin in his eighth year, he is able to reproduce apparently complete reading lists, and he recalls the precise routine of his French lessons and writing exercises. "As to my private reading, I can only speak of what I remember" (9)—yet he goes on to outline his readings in some detail.

There is considerable narrative distance, however, at least partially maintained by frequent references to writing time (book time): "At the point which I have now reached" (109), "It was at the period of my mental progress which I have now reached" (111). The reader is not tempted to immerse himself in past time but is continually reminded of the dramatic developmental scheme that forms the plot of the story. In the final, anticlimactic chapter on the "remainder" of Mill's life, of course, this sense of dramatic development recedes.

The narrator Mill mercilessly analyzes the young protagonist in his typically "objective" style. In spite of the great advantage of his unique education, the young Mill was denied parental love, had no friends, failed to develop manual dexterity, and so on. Victorian writers, perhaps through self-pity, often depict their past selves as pathetic little creatures, but Mill's straightforward unemotional prose style helps to create an especially vivid picture of a young man of "average" intelligence with a head start in education, equally significant deprivations, and a special status as "one of the very few examples, in this country, of one who has, not thrown off religious belief, but never had it" (28). The clarity of self-presentation is diminished in the final chapter as the protagonist has achieved the essential selfhood of the narrator and enters a "purely literary" phase of life

(156). (An exception to this generalization in the final chapter is Mill's anecdotes about his activities in national politics as MP.)

As in Newman's case, Mill's self-narrative is at points caught up in a larger narrative, that of the Utilitarian movement and Radical politics in general, though Mill foregrounds his individuality and avoidance of "sectarianism." Mill's narrative contains even fewer reminiscences dealing with friends and associates than does Newman's, but of course it does treat the two dominant personal relationships in his life. In describing his father in the early chapters, Mill very carefully weighs the strengths and weaknesses of his father's character with the same sort of apparent detachment that he uses in analyzing his young self, and his father's ideas with the "balanced" point of view he had used in his well-known essays on Bentham and Coleridge. Part of the drama of the narrative lies in his partial rejection of (but never total rebellion from) the influence of his father. Like later Victorian autobiographers with famous fathers, Mill strives to set the historical record straight and correct any apparent misconceptions concerning the man.[5] He does go on to make some inflated claims for his father, however, in the final two chapters:

> In the power of influencing by mere force of mind and character, the convictions and purposes of others, and in the strenuous exertion of that power to promote freedom and progress, he left, as far as my knowledge extends, no equal among men, and but one among women. (123)

As this passage demonstrates, Mill increasingly comes to compare his father to his wife Harriet, the other dominant figure in his life. That comparison probably influenced his evaluations of his father, for some of Mill's references to Harriet are exceedingly unrealistic and abstract: "I have often compared her . . . to Shelley: but in thought and intellect, Shelley . . . was but a child compared with what she ultimately became" (112); "What I owe, even intellectually, to her, is, in its detail, almost infinite" (113). As in the case of some writings by John Ruskin, the reader must make allowances for certain absurd passages if he is to appreciate Mill's *Autobiography* as a serious work. In structural terms, of course, the void left by the receding presence of his father is replaced by that of Harriet Taylor.

In closely identifying his later career with Harriet Taylor, the author-narrator's rhetorical strategy is to associate her with his later works in such a way that they "argue for" both her and him. Obviously his emphasis on the issue of women's rights toward the end of the book is closely connected with her memory. Stillinger's reading of the *Autobiography* itself as a collaboration is consistent with Mill's statements in the text that imply that all his later works should be read as collaborations, but to read any autobiography in this way is highly problematic.[6]

Like Newman, Mill, at the most basic level, is speaking to the English public. His unique background and status serve to provide a special perspective on the universal development of thought. However, his immediate audience is not as obviously analyzable into specific groups in spite of Mill's obvious role as an outspoken, atheistic controversialist, highly aware of political and philosophical factions and parties. Before and after his mental crisis, he identifies himself primarily as a reformer whose goal is the improvement of mankind. The difference after the crisis is that he has an emotional commitment to this role. However, there is very little resembling Newman's appeal to a concrete human community in the *Autobiography*, only the adulation of his wife and qualified esteem of his father.

As has been shown, Mill sees an intimate connection between his story and the story of mankind, and his book is implicitly prophetic in much the same way that Newman's is. The meaning of Mill's crisis and new formulation of philosophy is somewhat blunted in that his veneration of Harriet Taylor could hardly occupy the place of Newman's religion; nevertheless, Mill's self-history is firmly rooted in contemporary social history with claims to universal meaning.

Chapter 3

Robert Dale Owen, *Threading My Way: An Autobiography* (1874)

A rigid classification of British Victorian autobiographies would exclude Robert Dale Owen's *Threading My Way*, since the author was a citizen of the United States, where he had lived for a half-century by the time he wrote his autobiography. Nevertheless, during the first quarter century of his life, the time covered by the book, Owen was a British subject, and his portrait of childhood in the household of the renowned manufacturer and radical reformer Robert Owen matches that of any other autobiographer in terms of its potential interest to students of nineteenth-century British history and culture.[1] Within the context of radical reform movements of the age, Owen's autobiography invites comparison with that of Mill. Both men were groomed by their fathers to work for the "progress of mankind," though in somewhat different ways.

In terms of narrative structure, the book can be usefully compared to several of the other autobiographies under study. Like those by Mill and Gosse, it is a critical yet nostalgic "father and son" story. Like Ruskin's it contains scenes of past experience remembered with pleasure for their own sake. Owen incorporated many long passages that could be classified as genealogy, memoirs, reminiscences, travelogue, and social history, and yet through it all he tells a story of self-development. Although his story of personal development lacks the intensity and rhetorical focus of Newman's or Mill's, it does not, like Ruskin's, deny or undercut the conventions of the genre.

Today Robert Dale Owen is remembered chiefly as the son of Robert Owen, the British manufacturer, factory reformer, and social theorist. However, the son attained considerable personal success in American politics, serving in the Indiana legislature, 1836–38, and as a member of the United States Congress, 1843–47, where he sponsored the 1845 bill that established the Smithsonian Institution. He was also known for his political publications, particularly those on the subject of emancipation, and for his books on spiritualism. Thus when he agreed to William Dean Howells's suggestion in late 1872 that he write his autobiography for serial publication in the *Atlantic Monthly* (published in book form in 1874), Owen, five years from death, was known as something more than his father's son to his American audience.

In his long career he had undergone a remarkable series of metamorphoses. In 1825, as a youthful disciple of his radical but wealthy father, he plunged with enthusiasm into an experimental community in rural Indiana. Undaunted by the failure of his father's utopian schemes and those of his friend Frances Wright, he moved to New York City in 1829 and began to make a name for himself as a freethought militant. Among other activities, he edited the controversial *Free Enquirer* and published the infamous *Moral Physiology; or, A Brief and Plain Treatise on the Population Question* (1830), and he generally acquired associations with issues such as birth control and atheism that were to haunt him for the rest of his life. In 1833 he returned as a married man to New Harmony, where he evolved into a pragmatic Democratic politician whose success can be measured by his election first to the Indiana legislature and, later, to the United States Senate. Although he rejected his early idealism and developed moderate positions on manifest destiny and the extension of slave states, his stands on women's rights, educational reform, and other issues continually led him into controversy. He remained active in both state and national politics until 1853, when he received the political appointment of chargé to Naples (Kingdom of the Two Sicilies). By the time he returned to America in 1860, he had been converted to spiritualism. He became involved with prewar politics and fairly rapidly moved his position from moderate Democrat to "war" Democrat, and, finally, to radical Republican, making his own proposals for the emancipation of slaves and, later, Reconstruction.[2] In the last decade of his life, he intensified his study and promotion of spiritualism, though he avoided active participation in spiritualist organizations. When he began to write the autobiographical sketches, he had recently published the second of his two books on spiritualism. His continuing involvement in the movement was to lead to an embarrassing and highly publicized scandal concerning his stubborn endorsement, and then sudden renunciation, of the spiritualist medium Katie King, soon after the publication of *Threading My Way*.[3]

Thus, throughout his adult life Owen had been immersed in controversy. Moving from the chaotic and doomed rural society created by his father to the world of big city radicals, Owen not only acquired a public reputation for dangerous religious and social views but quarreled with fellow radicals, most notably with Frances Wright, from whom he became progressively estranged.[4] Back in Indiana, although he shed his extreme political and social views, the volatile nature of nineteenth-century American politics involved him in constant disputes, with his Whig opponents making effective use of his radical past, on occasion even reprinting portions of *Moral Physiology* for distribution to potential voters.[5] At the same time, his former associates from the New York days saw him as betraying his old ideals as he became more moderate. Even his significant role in founding the Smithsonian Institution was subsequently obscured as a result of political infighting.[6] His increasingly progressive position on emancipation during the war years alienated many of his former political allies in Indiana. His espousal of a sort of Christianized version of spiritualism in his late career was the crowning touch, arousing the suspicion or anger of various groups, from his old agnostic associates to conventional Christians. It is easy to see parallels between the problematic position of Owen and those of other controversial autobiographers such as Martineau and Ruskin. Like Ruskin, Owen chose to deemphasize the controversy and view the distant past with nostalgia.[7]

If one does not balk at the title's pun on the textile industry and can allow Owen his enthusiastic acceptance of phrenology and his allusions to an imminent breakthrough in man's knowledge of the spiritual world, one will find the book well written and deserving of more critical attention than it has received. Owen wrote twelve chapters, or "papers," as he calls them. They are of approximately equal length, with the exception of the final one, which serves as a short epilogue. The principal plot is the developing boyhood and young adulthood of Robert Dale Owen, through his first twenty-five years, a fragment of his life that he labels "the tentative years." At the end of this time, Owen begins a new life as a permanent resident and citizen of the United States. There is no traumatic break with the father, but the son has deliberately chosen to pursue an independent life in America rather than to succeed his father as head of New Lanark. Like certain other autobiographers, such as Edmund Gosse, Owen ends his autobiography at the first great turning point in his life. Although it changes the course of his life, this event as a function of the plot does not generate the sort of psychological and intellectual drama associated with Gosse's move to London or Newman's conversion.

Unlike Gosse, Owen does not claim that telling his father's story is his primary motive for writing; however, this is clearly one of his purposes, and his father's history is intertwined with his own. In a larger sense, Owen narrates his grandfather's and father's roles in the development of the textile industry and goes on to consider the implications of the Industrial Revolution as a whole.

Owen avoids the dry chronology associated with the opening chapters of those autobiographies which incorporate genealogical material; he uses personal anecdotes and reflections to introduce the story of his mother's father, David Dale, who in partnership with Richard Arkwright founded New Lanark, and then his father, the archetypal self-made man who made New Lanark the most famous company town in the world. The intrinsically interesting history of "pioneer workers in the richest mine ever opened to human enterprise" (31), that is, automation of the textile industry, and the touching story of Robert Owen's courtship of Miss Dale are tied to personal associations; for example, his grandfather's funeral "is, of all my childish recollections, one of the earliest and most distinct" (39).

Moving on to his "Boy-Life in a Scottish Country Seat," Owen in recollecting childhood memories chiefly focuses on his moral and religious development, his attempt to "convert" his deistic father to his mother's style of Presbyterianism, and finally his own decision to become a "Universalist." Another foregrounded incident in the boy's self-development is his overhearing a conversation between two men in which he is praised (his father's rule was never to openly praise or blame him), an event that inspired him to adopt a more positive attitude toward life. This incident fairly early in the narrative introduces an idea that will be developed later: that his father, in spite of his good intentions, possessed an inadequate understanding of human psychological and spiritual needs. After devoting a chapter to the description of "that remarkable man, my father" and his methods, he continues with a more loosely organized chronicle of his boyhood life "at Braxfield and in London," including recollections of a visit to New Lanark by the Grand Duke Nicholas of Russia. His "early literary pretensions" foreshadow his later development in a general way.

Within the quarter-century span of time covered by his autobiography, Owen's experience at Emmanuel von Fellenberg's "self-governing college" at Hofwyl, Switzerland, is presented as the most significant "turning-point." All of chapter 5, which describes the college episode, could be described as an idyll, located roughly in the middle of the book. Aware that his account of this student-governed institution of learning must seem hopelessly idealistic, he writes:

> All this sounds, I dare say, strangely Utopian and extravagant. As I write, it seems to myself so widely at variance with a thirty years' experience of public life, that I should scruple, at this distance of time, to record it, if I had not, forty years ago, carefully noted down my recollections while they were still fresh and trustworthy. (155)

At any rate, Owen reports that he left Hofwyl not only "perfectly well, but athletic (having overcome a weak and nervous constitution)" (169) and with an "abiding faith in human virtue and in social progress" (175).

The college years are followed by an almost equally idyllic journey down the Rhine and a stay at the estate of Baron von Munchausen near Hanover, where the youthful protagonist becomes enamored of the Baron's beautiful daughter, in one of several potential love affairs described in the book. But Owen ends the chapter with a continuation of the story of his father's fortunes.

Although the father was doing well in business, his reputation and influence as a radical reformer was receding. Owen once again analyzes his father's faults: his lack of "thorough culture" in youth, his failure to understand the spiritual needs of mankind. Although this critique is given from the point of view of the retrospective narrator, it signals a growing distance between the protagonist and his father and reinforces the significance of the Hofwyl experience as a turning point in the protagonist's developing independence.

His seventh chapter, "Educating a Wife," is in a sense a self-contained story. "Jessie" is the pseudonym for a precocious, pretty, ten-year-old New Lanark girl taken in by the Owen family. Owen, at the age of twenty years, was responsible for this arrangement because he wanted to groom her to be his future bride. Because of her extreme youth and the potential objections of his parents, he revealed his intention only to his sister Anne, who promised to help in the secret scheme. As he became involved in his father's experiment in New Harmony, Indiana (explained more fully in the following chapters), he developed the idea of settling down with Jessie in America. He had determined to propose to the girl before leaving for America in 1827 (when she was thirteen), but when he at last confided in his mother, she persuaded him to wait three more years, and by the end of that time, Jessie had married another man. In a rare glimpse outside the time frame of the story, Owen reports a poignant meeting with Jessie over thirty years later in which they for the first and only time discussed their love for one another.

Owen describes his part in the history of New Harmony in "The Social Experiment at New Harmony" and "My Experience of Communal Life," chapters 8 and 9. He narrates his own immediate, instinctive adaptations to American life and continues to analyze his father's strengths and weaknesses as a reformer, the potential success of the cooperative movement, and the positive and negative effects of the Industrial Revolution.

After the failure of New Harmony, Owen became involved with another doomed communal enterprise, the Nashoba, Tennessee, community organized by Frances Wright. He later traveled to Paris with Wright, and chapters 10 and 11 are composed largely of reminiscences of his meetings with "interesting people" in Paris and London—General Lafayette, Mary Shelley, and various public sensations of the time, including the phrenologist Spurzheim, the reformer Rowland Hill (responsible for the penny post), and the poet Letitia Elizabeth Landon.

The short, final chapter provides closure: "Here ends the first portion of my life, during which my home was in the Old World and in my native land. These were the tentative years, the years throughout which I was proving all things and seeking for that which is good" (360).

Like Mill's narrative, Owen's tells a story of self-development and simultaneous movement away from, but no final break with, a powerful father, but because the story ends only with the "new beginning" in America, the protagonist never becomes the author-narrator, although he anticipates him. Though Owen's tone is much more nostalgic than Mill's and his story more distanced, *Threading My Way* is just as surely imbued with history and prophecy. The story of New Lanark, New Harmony, and the Owenite movement in general is part of popular history, and the dynamics of industrial and social change provides a still larger frame of narrative. Owen's spiritualist vision is only hinted at in this story of early self-development, but his critique of industrialism, capitalism, and reformist theory provides a certain prophetic element. Overall, Owen's view of history is one of gradual improvement through technological development coupled with moral progress through social reform. His narrative of self-development is similarly based on the gradual accumulation of wisdom.

> In looking back upon myself as I was in those days, I have often wondered how far my after-life might have been affected by the judicious advice of some cool-headed, dispassionate friend ... what, for example, the result would have been if the Robert Dale Owen of seventy could have become the counsellor of the Robert Dale Owen of twenty-five." (296)

This passage, which incorporates a narrative method similar to that of Charles Dickens in *Great Expectations*, illustrates the friendly, ironic distance between the author-narrator and his idealistic and immature protagonist. Significantly, Owen continues by discussing the cultivated but zealous reformer Frances Wright, who might have been his mentor but who unfortunately lacked common sense (as well as sexual appeal). Having left his home because of his extraordinary but flawed father, perhaps in his early adulthood he was looking for his own Harriet Taylor. His later portrait of Mary Shelley as a supremely sympathetic, wise lady suggests that he may have thought of her as potentially filling such a role.

In spite of the book's overall detached tone and ironic distance, the narrator at a few points late in the narrative, as the protagonist approaches adulthood, reveals an increasing need to defend himself against the perception that he is a "visionary dreamer" (336), undoubtedly alluding to his association with the idealist Owenite reform tradition, American radical politics, and the spiritualist movement.

"Since one purpose of an autobiography is to furnish to its readers materials for a thorough acquaintance with the autobiographer" (333), the narrator compares two cranial charts of himself, prepared independently by two prominent phrenologists, which agree in showing "Causality" or reasoning power as one of the "predominant organs" of his brain and "Marvelousness" as one of its smallest (336). He promises a later autobiographical account dealing with his "Connection, many years later in life, with the spiritual movement, [and then] there will be means of judging whether my opinion touching intercommunion between two phases of human existence is based on logical premises, or is due to a love of the marvelous, outrunning practical experience and sound discretion" (336).[8]

In spite of this defensiveness near the end of the book, the narrator handles the story of his youthful protagonist's self-development rather lightly, with little interior drama or tension between internal and external reality. Even in criticizing his father's beliefs, Owen applies the reflective perspective of the narrator without describing an historical conflict between the protagonist and his father. Potentially the most dramatic revelation of inner experience in the book concerns the story of "Jessie," the young girl Owen planned to make his wife.

The motive he gives for relating the story of his "secret love" is notable for its appeal to a sort of modified "confessional" convention that is not prominent in Victorian autobiography:

> Here let me confess that it needed, as prompting motive to overcome the natural reluctance one feels to confide to the public such details of inner life as one has seldom given even to intimate friends, a sense of the duty which an autobiographer owes his readers. They are entitled . . . to whatever of interest or value is strictly his own to relate; the secrets of others, however, not being included in that category. (232)

Nevertheless, aside from this embedded story of thwarted romance, which has the structure of a realistic short story, nothing in the autobiography can be classified as a dramatic revelation of inner experience. The dominant quality of Owen's autobiography is not that of a dramatic attempt to recover inner experience but rather an entertaining recital of observation and anecdotes. Whether he is retelling the inherited story of his grandfather Dale's amusing dispute with his partner Richard Arkwright, relating his conversation with his father on the subject of world religion, or giving the short Dickensian tale of the "English Mail Coach" in order to illustrate the English character (353–58), Owen freely uses fictional techniques to dramatize the story and reports dialogue in direct quotations (much as Gosse will do in *Father and Son*), in situations where he could not possibly remember exactly what had been said. Very rarely does he refer to a loss or possible distortion of memory, but much of the content of his somewhat episodic autobiography is as arbitrary as that of Ruskin's *Praeterita* will be.

Owen's handling of past time in *Threading My Way* is also in some ways similar to Ruskin's. The narrator indulges himself in recalling isolated childhood scenes that he associates with beauty and pleasure, and the prose is laden with sensuous visual imagery. A visit to Rosebank, his grandfather's country seat on the Clyde River, is recalled in an elaborate description of "its trees, its flowers, its mystical paths, all its accessories and its surroundings, like none other on earth" (41). And the related description of a childhood "love affair" with "a certain little maid" from a neighborhood farmhouse is delivered in a quiet, wistful tone.

Aside from his self-presentation as a sane and rational man, Owen's chief rhetorical purpose in the book is to

> estimate at its just value, and no more, the character of that remarkable man, my father. Perhaps no one has been more favorably situated than I to judge him fairly and dispassionately. His child, but not (except during my youth) . . . his "disciple,"— the partiality of a son is so far corrected by the scruples of a dissenter, that I hope to avoid alike the weakness of eulogy and the error of extenuation. (89)

Owen not only describes his father's character but devotes long passages to analyzing his father's ideas—both in the early, highly successful phase of experiments at New Lanark and height of his public reputation as a reformer and in the later failures in America and loss of public esteem toward the end of the time period covered by the book (the mid-1820s). Indeed Owen's portrait of his father does appear to be carefully balanced. At the heart of the son's critique is the observation that Robert Owen, in spite of his genuine love for mankind, his willingness to make personal sacrifices (he ultimately lost most of his considerable fortune in the New Harmony project), and the irrepressible optimism that he maintained to the end of his life, was hampered by a relative ignorance both of the history of ideas and the complex psychological and spiritual needs of mankind. Unlike Gosse's scathing indictment of his father's religious beliefs and way of life, Owen's critique of his well-intentioned father seems mild, especially in light of his father's increasingly impractical and eccentric behavior in the later stages of his career. Owen modifies and corrects his father's extreme, secularized "millenialist" views, naive faith in human nature, and simplistic, deterministic views of education and, in a broader sense, he analyzes the failure of industrialism to improve the material welfare of the worker. He offers his own, temperate but positive, views of the cooperative movement and the possibility of moral progress for mankind. But Owen's strategy for distancing himself from his father is more subtle and complex than its surface appearance.

The protagonist's evolving relationship with his father is similar to that seen in Mill's autobiography. Young Owen's task is to follow in the footsteps of the father up to a certain point and then to criticize and refine the father's ideas in developing his own philosophy. Owen comes to America as his father's assistant, and even after he begins to live an independent life, in a sense he is carrying on his father's work in his continuing involvement in political, economic, and social reform. It is true, however, that, despite the discourse in which Owen, like Mill, reinforces the reputation of his father, the father is decisively displaced in the narrative. As the son establishes his identity as an American, his father's fortunes fall.

The father loses more than four-fifths of his total wealth as he stubbornly persists in his attempt to make a success of his doomed social experiment in America (293). Even more significantly, the father's reputation as a social reformer continues to decline as his ideas are increasingly seen as impractical and eccentric. Although the father is not completely ruined and in fact maintains his irrepressible optimism, the plot line of his story is nevertheless tragic, while the son's is comic.

At this point we may remind ourselves that Owen writes as an old man whose life has undergone several important turning points beyond that which closes his "tentative years" at the end of his autobiography. It is true that he leaves his youthful protagonist at the beginning of an exciting new life that will be largely independent from the influence of his father. And Owen as narrator does not exaggerate the declining reputation of his father. There is abundant evidence that in his declining years, after the final failure of the American experiment, Robert Owen increasingly impressed his contemporaries as a persistent bore who merely repeated his old ideas. Nevertheless, the aesthetic or dramatic distance between father and son in *Threading My Way* relies partially on an implicit distortion of historical chronology. By the time Robert Owen died in 1858, he had been involved in the spiritualist movement for several years. In fact, in the summer of 1853, when Owen heard of his father's conversion to spiritualism, he wrote to a friend that he regretted "as every judicious friend must, the strange infatuation which has overtaken my good father."[9] Then when he visited his father in England on his way to take his post as chargé in Naples in autumn of 1853, he attended one or two spiritualist séances at his father's insistence, but, at that time, remained unconvinced.[10] Four years later, Owen was seriously studying spiritualist phenomena, and his decision to write his first book on spiritualism roughly coincided with his father's death. In moving from agnosticism to spiritualism, Owen was, once again, following his father, whether or not the move can be attributed to direct influence. When Owen, as narrator of his autobiography, criticizes his father's essential secularism up until old age (193), he could be criticizing himself. One of the most striking aspects of his curious stance is that Owen the narrator makes no serious or sustained attempt to describe the intellectual development of his youthful protagonist, nor does he set forth his mature, "book time" ideas in any depth, with the exception of modifying and criticizing the opinions of his father and making broad generalizations about the effects of the Industrial Revolution. One effect is that Owen implicitly concedes his status as "Robert Owen's son"—this in spite of his reputation as a controversialist, a man of ideas. As previously pointed out, Owen only hints at his role as an advocate for spiritualism, and his anecdote about rejecting his mother's Presbyterianism in his youth ("from that day I became a Universalist," 88) obscures the secularism and agnosticism of his middle years.

The author-narrator's distinctively American identity as one aspect of his relationship with his audience in *Threading My Way* offers an obvious contrast to the other autobiographies under study. Throughout the book, he addresses an American reader, and sometimes makes special attempts to explain his Scottish and English upbringing. Brought up in an atmosphere of Scottish nationalism, Owen as a child visited Wallace's Cave, the secluded retreat of that legendary chieftain: "No Fourth-of-July oration, no visit to Plymouth Rock, ever produced, on young scion of Puritan, a deeper impression than did the sight of this narrow, secluded cell upon me" (74). Yet there is no doubt about the American identity of the narrator who at the age of twenty-four had landed for the first time in "the Canaan of my hopes" (264): "Despite their shortcomings, I like the English. Theirs is not the highest character, but it has noble elements" (350). "Like us, their legitimate descendants, the English exhibit a self-sufficiency somewhat of the Pharisaical stamp. . . . they are estimable rather than amiable, and their perceptions of justice are quicker than their emotions of mercy" (350–51). Owen's father was ethnically English (though with Welsh roots), his mother Scottish. By implication Owen contrasts his American identity with the English identity of his father.

Owen works to establish a narrative voice that is not only pleasantly garrulous and unpretentious but reasonable and rational. As a zealous radical reformer in his youth, he never approached the ludicrous eccentricity of the mysterious American described as the "Page of Nature, All in Green" (265–67) nor of the more foolish members of the New Harmony community. As a mature, retired statesman and writer, Owen implies that his seemingly "wild belief" that "occasional intervention from another world in this is not a superstitious delirium, but a grand reality" (336) will be vindicated. At any rate, his self-history, unlike Newman's, deals only with a distant youth and does not approach this important "conversion."

Finally, Owen's history of his early life serves as a "document" much the same as do the autobiographies of Mill and Gosse: it documents the development of the textile industry, which played such a crucial role in the history of British industrialism, and the radical reform movement in which his father was a prime mover. It also helps to document the dramatic transitions in individuals and cultures as they continued to move westward across the Atlantic in the nineteenth century.

Chapter 4

Harriet Martineau, *Autobiography* (1877)

Harriet Martineau's two-volume autobiography is one of the longer ones to be discussed in this study,[1] yet she wrote both volumes during a remarkably brief three-month span in 1855, while she was suffering from an extended period of illness that she believed would end in her death.[2] In fact Martineau went on to live another twenty-one years, and busy years at that, principally occupied by writing leaders for the *Daily News*. The *Autobiography* was published soon after her death, so that the *ex morte* stance of the narrator is appropriate, but it is as if Mill had not revised and brought up to date his text of 1853–54, which was also prompted by a premature expectation of death: the contemporary reader could see that Martineau's narrative, presented as a full life and career autobiography, ended about two decades too soon.

However, regardless of Martineau's motives for not extending her autobiography, we see that what may appear in retrospect to be an especially open-ended narrative is really quite conventional in form. Volume 2 had brought Martineau up to the time of her maturity as a writer and a thinker. All her "transitional" work was behind her by 1855, and so was the development of her opinions, her philosophy of life. By 1855, Martineau had already entered into the "final" journalistic stage of her writing career and was writing leaders for the *Daily News*. The implication of Martineau's decision not to extend the 1855 manuscript after her recovery is that both the narrator and the protagonist (at the end of the narrative) can be identified with the public image of the woman who died in 1876.

Martineau's autobiography is squarely in the tradition of Gibbon's life and career model. Like Gibbon, Mill, and many others, she believes that because of her "remarkable" life, she has a "duty," an "obligation" to publish her life story (1:1). In her introduction,[3] she emphasizes her decision *not* to publish her correspondence and contrasts the essentially private nature of correspondence (though, she insists, there is nothing in the letters which could damage her reputation) with the public nature of the autobiography. Though letters are *written*, they are bound by the same "laws of honour" that govern private conversation. Here Martineau concisely articulates the conventional Victorian division between private and public spheres and implicitly valorizes the public discourse of the autobiography by refusing to publish that private discourse which usually is not intended for publication when it is written.[4]

Like Mill's, Martineau's narrative covers the full course of life up until the time of writing—with an emphasis on the formation of beliefs and opinions and the history of publications—but she includes much more detail than does Mill,[5] dividing her life into major periods, which are broken down further into sections, a formal method similar to that which will be employed by Spencer and one that encourages a persistently chronological approach, though in the text there is some jumping forward and backward in time. "Period 1" begins with Martineau's earliest childhood memories and carries the protagonist to the age of eight. Martineau was born into a middle-class family in Norwich, the sixth of eight children. Her father was a local manufacturer, and he and his wife were Unitarians who held progressive views, including the belief that girls as well as boys should be educated. However, the dominant characteristic of Martineau's early life was her ill health. Like many other Victorian autobiographers, Martineau recalls a miserable childhood, and her child protagonist already suffers from that scourge of Victorian writers—a "nervous" disorder (1:10). She felt unattractive and rejected, her sensitive nature misunderstood or ignored by her parents. The following statement by Martineau is especially representative of Victorian narratives of childhood: "I am sure that a little more of the cheerful tenderness which was in those days thought bad for children, would have saved me from my worst faults, and from a world of suffering" (1:11). Much like little Robert Dale Owen, Martineau "had no self-respect, and an unbounded need of approbation and affection." The self-deprecation is also typical: "I was a dull, unobservant, slow, awkward child" (1:23). As for her mental qualities, the child protagonist is intensely religious and fond of giving moral advice, and she composes a sermon. Reinforcing a retrospective point of view, the narrator comments on the protagonist's childish awe of ministers and clergymen, a "remnant" of which persists in the adult's consciousness, in spite of her mature view "that the intellectual and moral judgment of priests of all persuasions is inferior to that of any other order of men" (1:32). By the end of the first period of the narrative, the narrator has already made it clear that the protagonist's development will involve a movement from a religious to a scientific or positivistic vision. Among other interior events in this part is Martineau's first "political" interest, the death of Nelson.

In the narrative of the second period, from age eight to seventeen, Martineau continues to emphasize the development of her mind, which has become "desperately methodical." Her own analysis of the Bible led her to a "great step in the process of thought and knowledge,—that whereas Judaism was a perceptive religion, Christianity was mainly a religion of principles,—or assumed to be so." From her parents (who had shed the old Calvinistic French Huguenot faith of the Martineaus) she inherited a mild, dull Unitarianism, based on "shallow" scholarship, which did not include the concept of Hell (1:42). Her discovery and subsequent fascination with the intellectual vigor of Milton's *Paradise Lost* in retrospect "must have been my first experience of moral relief through intellectual resource" (1:43). In this portion of the narrative Martineau describes one "learning experience" after another: a visit to the country for reasons of health in 1811 gave her the opportunity to transplant some wild strawberry roots, "the first putting my hand in among the operations of Nature, to modify them" (1:50); her passionate affection for her new baby sister Ellen led her to a kind of obsession with her childhood development; her home lessons in Latin and mathematics from her brothers gave way to instruction at a day school. Her attendance with her sister Rachel at the day school of the Rev. Isaac Perry led to a "new state of happiness" (1:62). Her progress in school was rapid and led to the discovery of an intellectual life in which she found, as she will find for the rest of her life, "refuge from suffering, and an always unexhausted spring of moral strength and enjoyment" (1:65).

Unfortunately, Perry's school was closed two years later, and Martineau was becoming increasingly deaf, an affliction that, exacerbated by her parents' misunderstanding, heightened what seems to have been an already neurotic self-consciousness. However, by reading the *Globe* and the Unitarian periodical *Monthly Repository*, along with her home lessons, she "was all the while becoming a political economist without knowing it, and, at the same time, a sort of walking Concordance of Milton and Shakespeare" (1:72). At the age of sixteen, she was sent for a time to the school of her aunt in Bristol, the chief benefit of which seems to have been the kindness and understanding of Aunt Kentish herself, who became a kind of substitute for Martineau's mother. (Martineau reports that during this phase of her life she habitually lied to her mother out of fear.) It was at Bristol, however, that Martineau reached the height of her religious fanaticism and pastor worship, "a stage which I should probably have had to pass through at any rate" (1:96).

Embedded in Martineau's account of the "second period" are numerous references to her later writing career that strongly foreshadow what is to come. Bad handwriting, along with deafness and unmanageable hair, is one of the "griefs" of her early life, but we are told that it was later to improve and that "[i]f anyone had told me then how many reams of paper I should cover in the course of my life, life would have seemed a sort of purgatory to me" (1:90). We are also informed that portions of her childhood have been "elsewhere narrated" in publications by Martineau (1:50, 59, 60), that her first publication was going to appear in the *Monthly Repository* (1:71), and that family discussions of the Battle of Waterloo were ironic in light of her later essay "History of the Thirty Years' Peace" (1:81).

Of the third period of her life, which carries her to the age of thirty, Martineau writes: "These thirteen years, extending from my entering on womanhood to my complete establishment in an independent position, as to occupation and the management of my own life, seem to form a marked period of themselves" (1:97). Herein are the central turning points in her narrative of development, both in terms of inner events (opinions, life philosophy) and outer events (first publication, first successful publication). Bolstered by an especially good relationship with her mother and other family members at this time, Martineau enthusiastically forged her identity as a scholar and writer, in spite of her increasing deafness and her consciousness that her line of activity was not conventional for young ladies, at least not for young ladies in provincial towns (1:100). (In this last respect she compares herself to Jane Austen.) Martineau catalogs her accomplishments in a manner very like that of Mill.

Taking up a "strange passion" for translating, she tackled Tacitus's *Life of Agricola* and produced a translation that she thought superior to that of John Aikin. She studied the Bible "incessantly and immensely" and, inspired by the work of the Rev. Lant Carpenter,[6] conceived of a book describing the Jews "under the immediate expectation of the Messiah," a work that became second only to *Eastern Life* (1848) in her affections when she wrote and published it years later (1:103). She also immersed herself in the works of John Locke, Joseph Priestley, and David Hartley, from whose *Scholia* she derived "earnest desire of self-discipline, and devotion to duty" (1:105). When she was about twenty, some remarks from her brother James ("then my oracle") regarding his first session at York College led her to her own formulation of the "Necessarian" doctrine—that "all the workings of the universe are governed by laws which cannot be broken by human will" (1:109). The concept of free will is only a superstitious remnant. Not only did this conviction become the intellectual key to her work, the "main-spring of my activity," but

> I can truly say that if I have had the blessing of any available strength under sorrow, perplexity, sickness and toil, during a life which has been any thing but easy, it is owing to my repose upon eternal and irreversible laws, working in every department of the universe, without any interference from any random will, human or divine. (1:111)

Although she held on for many years to a progressively weaker form of what seemed in retrospect the pseudo-Christianity of her Unitarian upbringing, she soon applied her new doctrine to the New Testament and concluded that it "proceeds on the ground of necessarian, rather than free-will doctrine" (1:112).

At the instigation of her brother James, Martineau in 1821 submitted "Female Writers on Practical Divinity" to the editor of the *Monthly Repository*. Although the author-narrator says she is now ashamed of the content of that paper, she remarks: "There is certainly something entirely peculiar in the sensation of seeing one's self in print for the first time:—the lines burn themselves in upon the brain in a way of which black ink is incapable, in any other mode" (1:119). Recalling her eldest brother's admiration of her article, Martineau writes, "That evening made me an authoress" (1:120). At the same time, her mode of writing—careful drafts with little or no revision—was now set for life (1:122).

Even the series of tragedies that came in the early 1820s—a sudden increase in her deafness, the decline and death of a beloved brother, the decline and death of her father, the madness and suicide of the only suitor she was ever to have, the financial catastrophe that wiped out the Martineau family fortune—all of these things seemed to strengthen rather than diminish her literary ambitions. The financial crisis was, ironically, liberating, because with the loss of fortune came the loss of restrictions associated with gentility, and Martineau was more than ever free to fashion an independent, unconventional life for herself. The loss of her suitor left her "mind . . . wholly free from all idea of love-affairs" and left her free to follow her "business in life": "to think and learn, and to speak out with absolute freedom what I have thought and learned" (1:133).

In 1827 Martineau began to publish a few stories with "the solemn old Calvinistic publisher Houlston" (her first "pecuniary success"), including some on issues related to political economy, even before she became familiar with that term by reading Jane Marcet's *Conversations on Political Economy* (1:138).[7] At the same time, she continued to publish articles in the *Monthly Repository*, whose new, Unitarian editor, William James Fox, and his friends offered her help and encouragement. In 1831, her literary enterprises led her to London, where she boarded with a cousin for a time before reluctantly returning home to her mother.

The second "great event" of her writing career—the first being her first publication—is her winning all three prizes in an essay-writing competition for the best Unitarian tracts aimed at Catholics, Jews, and Mohammedeans. "I had now found that I could write, and I might rationally believe that authorship was my legitimate career" (1:156). Ironically, the author-narrator pauses in her narrative here to explain that she repudiates the content of those essays, having long ago totally rejected the "dreamy way of metaphysical accommodation" with Unitarianism expressed in them (1:158–59). By this time Martineau was already planning the "Political Economy Series" of stories that would secure her public recognition and financial success.

Martineau portrays her twenty-nine-year-old protagonist as an obsessive, relentless writer with an absolute commitment to her project. Her proposal for the series was rejected by one publisher after another until she was able to secure a relatively unfavorable agreement with Charles, the brother of William James Fox, to publish the works by subscription, with a minimum of five hundred copies for the first run. Fox nearly abandoned the project, which seemed doomed to failure, but instead, the first number was an instant success that sold thousands of copies. The author-narrator proclaims that from the moment she received the letter of 10 February 1832 with the initial good news from Fox "my cares were over.... From that hour I have never had any other anxiety about employment than what to choose, nor any real care about money" (1:178). This is a decisive moment in the narrative:

> I cannot but know that in my life there has been a great waste of precious time and material; but I had now, by thirty years of age, ascertained my career, found occupation, and achieved independence; and thus the rest of my life was provided with its duties and its interests. (1:181)

She was now able to make a permanent move to London, where she was later joined by her mother and her aunt.

Martineau packs the lengthy period 4, which takes her protagonist to the age of thirty-seven, with detailed descriptions of her writing habits, her reflections on writing and writers, and portraits of people she met in London; not surprisingly, the pace of the narrative of development is considerably slackened. Her writing schedule for producing the monthly series of political economy tales is nearly as precise as that which will be given by Trollope for his novels, and in her case, it includes time for research and a logical outline of each subject (1:193–95). She relates the circumstances in which she wrote various individual tales (all of which are more or less didactic and promote a point of view consistent with laissez-faire economics). She sets the record straight on the controversy surrounding her "Malthusian" story, "The Population Question"—ridiculed in an unsigned article in the *Quarterly Review* (1:204–8)—and relates various other anecdotes about her trials and tribulations as a somewhat controversial author in the London literary world. Referring to rumors that she had been secretly married, that her supposed patron Lord Brougham had actually written many of her books, and others, she writes, "I hope this Memoir will discredit all the absurd reports which may yet be connected with my station and my doings in life" (1:218). One political theme running throughout is her criticism of Whig politicians:[8] "Whiggism has become mere death in life,—a mere transitional state, now nearly worn out" (1:214). Portraits of fellow intellectuals and writers can be biting; for example, "Robert Owen is not the man to think differently of a book for having read it" (1:233). Most of all, Martineau describes her persistent effort to keep to the rigorous schedule to which she had committed herself, despite interludes of debilitating illness, and the anxiety about the reception of each published tale. In a retrospective commentary the author-narrator reports that she lately has calculated her total income from publications at the time of writing the autobiography to be about ten thousand pounds, but "[t]here is nothing in money that could pay me for the pain of the slightest deflexion from my own convictions, or the most trifling restraint on my freedom of thought and speech" (1:268).

After completing the final tale for her successful series, Martineau set out to travel in America during the period 1834–36, but the author-narrator defers her description of this journey to reprint "the bulk of an article on 'Literary Lionism,' written in 1837, which will show, better than anything which I can now relate, how I regarded the flatteries of a drawing-room while living in the midst of them" (1:271). This enormous section (164 pages in the original edition) can be described as memoirs and reminiscences about dozens of public personalities (primarily authors) whom Martineau met in London: at this point, not only the chronological narrative of "inner development" but also that of "outer events" is at a standstill. Martineau organizes her essay around the theme of the relationship between writers and the public and, in particular, the vanity of writers when exposed to public adulation.

Following this thematic section, Martineau once again takes up a chronological account, describing her travels in America, including meeting with political figures such as John Marshall, Daniel Webster, Henry Clay, and Andrew Jackson, and literary figures such as Ralph Waldo Emerson and Margaret Fuller, with whom she had an ambivalent relationship. Her generally positive reception was blunted, however, when she joined the abolitionist group surrounding William Lloyd Garrison and became outspoken against slavery in public meetings. Appealing to her book *Society in America* (1837) as the primary record of what she saw and thought about America, Martineau focuses on the controversial issue of her relationship with the abolitionists. "In this place I feel it right to tell my story.... [I]t will stand as a record of what really took place, in answer to some false reports and absurd misrepresentations" (2:8). Her main concern in this apologia is to show that her opinions follow from principle and observation of fact rather than a predilection to meddle in American affairs.

After the protagonist Martineau's arrival back in England, the narrative once more is dominated by the chronology of her publications. First, there is the story of publishing her American books—*Society in America* and *Retrospect of Western Travels*—which becomes a sort of moralistic tale about the publishing industry: "it may be well to show how the degradation of literature comes about, in times when speculating publishers try to make grasping authors, and to convert the serious function of authorship into a gambling match" (2:100). She was beset by unscrupulous publishers who urged her to write the book for strictly commercial reasons, with no care for the quality of her ideas, but she finally found the reputable firm of Saunders and Otley. (She was amazed when even Saunders assumed—wrongly—that she would request favorable notices of the book from acquaintances.) As she was finishing her book, Martineau was faced with a momentous decision: should she accept the editorship of a new journal of economics? After "painful vacillation" she let the negative advice from her brother James carry the day and turned to the writing of her novel *Deerbrook*. A description of Queen Victoria's coronation ("The festival was a highly barbaric one, to my eyes." [2:127]) is followed by her first visit to the Lake District and then a European tour, which ended in her succumbing to the mysterious "internal" disease that prostrated her: she was placed under the care of Thomas Greenhow, her physician brother-in-law at Newcastle-upon-Tyne, and "from that neighborhood I did not move for six years" (2:146).[9] This was the end of "the anxious period during which my reputation, and my industry, and my social intercourse were at the height of their prosperity; but which was so charged with troubles that when I lay down on my couch of pain ... I felt myself comparatively happy in my release from responsibility, anxiety, and suspence" (2:146).

Martineau's fifth period takes her to the age of forty-three, and it focuses on her illness of 1839–44. In terms of the autobiography's narrative flow, it is as though a long period of physical journeys (dominated by the travels in America) suddenly gives way to a time when the body is nearly static while the mind moves—especially the unconscious mind, apparently. (Martineau says she alternated her position between bed and sofa, and she refused to travel at all, even on the advice of her brother-in-law to seek medical advice in London.) Just as the third period of age seventeen to age thirty concludes with the chief turning point in the narrative of Martineau's career as the successful producer of literary texts, this fifth period concludes with the chief turning point in the narrative of Martineau's development of mind.

At the beginning Martineau announces that her narrative will be short because she has already given an account of this time in her book *Life in the Sick-Room* (1844), a move that reinforces the already close bond between life story and publication record. Martineau was now liberated from the company of her mother, who was relocated in Liverpool, near three of her children, and her aunt, who died—she explains that her resumption of caring for them after her return from America had contributed to the "excessive anxiety of mind" and the "extreme tension of nerves" that led to her breakdown (2:150–52).[10] Martineau sought and found the partial isolation and monotony she desired, but of course, she continued to write, not only her sickroom book, which emphasizes the mental anguish suffered by any invalid, but also *The Man and the Hour* (a historical novel about the Haitian revolutionary Toussaint L'Ouverture), and a series of children's tales. *Life in the Sick-Room* allowed her to give vent to the hidden suffering she felt (the first edition was published anonymously) but in retrospect appears morbid, evidence that Martineau was still "lingering in the metaphysical stage of mind." In general, during the 1839–44 period, however, the protagonist's meditations on life, death, and religion were leading her to shed her old "metaphysical" beliefs and adopt a stance of philosophical atheism (2:188–89).

At about the middle of the fifth period, Martineau began to be attracted to the practice of mesmerism as a possible cure for her illness and after a series of inquiries arranged for a series of treatments beginning in the summer of 1844 (both for herself and for Jane, the sickly girl who kept her company), which were remarkably successful. There is very little narrative here, except for reference to the cure itself and to its considerable effects. Martineau the protagonist nearly disappears; instead, the incident is described in retrospect by the author-narrator in terms of the controversy surrounding it and then in terms of the extraordinary changes it effected in Martineau's life. The reader is referred to yet another publication, *Letters on Mesmerism* (1845), for an actual description of the sessions that cured Martineau. The controversies over Martineau's association with and publication about mesmerism extend beyond those that have become almost routine in her controversial life: it is not simply a case of her quarrel with the editor of the *Atheneum,* which originally published the *Letters.* From this time Martineau's commitment to mesmerism became an integral part of her personal version of philosophical atheism. Nor is the controversy confined to the public arena: Martineau's estrangement from some close friends and family members, including her favorite brother James, will be related to her new beliefs.[11]

Martineau's account of her ten-year sixth period, to the age of fifty-three, begins with a summary that serves to shape her narrative of self-development:

> My life, it has been seen, began with winter. Then followed a season of storm and sunshine, merging in a long gloom. If I had died of that six years' illness, I should have considered my life a fair average one, as to happiness,—even while thinking more about happiness and caring more for it. . . . But the spring, summer, and autumn of life were yet to come. I have had them all now,—all rapidly succeeding each other, and crowded into a small space, like the Swedish summer. (2:203)

Of course this plot of personal happiness and satisfaction is inseparable from the new intellectual insights that have come to Martineau along with her full acceptance of mesmerism and a purely atheistic philosophy: "The objective and disinterested contemplation of eternity is, in my apprehension, the sublimest pleasure that human faculties are capable of" (2:208).

Freed from her illness, Martineau launched into a newly active life, visiting the Lake District and other areas to see her relatives. She also meets Henry G. Atkinson, "whose friendship has been the great privilege of the concluding period of my life" (2:213). Although, as Martineau is careful to point out, Atkinson was not the person who mesmerized her in her illness, he came into her life at exactly the right moment to function as the final, personal influence leading her to her mature final stage of development (in every sense, as Martineau believes that she is dying as she writes). "I owe my recovery mainly to him . . . my ten last happy years have been his gift to me" (2:213), writes Martineau, but he is much more than a personal friend; he is a prophet, much underrated and misunderstood by the public, who leads her to reject all metaphysics forever and fully accept positivism.

Since the last ten-year period represents her final, completed stage of development, it is not surprising that the chronology of events here is not always clear. The protagonist has reached her goal and has become the mature Martineau who is author of the autobiography. She describes her move to Ambleside, in the Lake District, and the house she built there, as well as her sometimes uneasy relations with her new neighbors. She includes anecdotes about her famous neighbor William Wordsworth and the visiting Margaret Fuller and Ralph Waldo Emerson, among others, and describes her relationship with Charlotte Brontë. A trip to the Middle East resulted in one of the three book publications foregrounded in this final section: *Eastern Life* (1848), which focuses on the religious development of the region. In discussing the key idea upon which she bases the book, she gives in effect another narrative summary of her own development, at a highly abstract level. Each individual, like each people, passes through a metaphysical, then a theological stage, before reaching a still higher stage (2:280). This of course sounds very much like Comtean philosophy; in 1851 she read and successfully translated into English Comte's *Positive Philosophy* (1853). She describes the translation—and condensation—of Comte's work as the most pleasant task she ever had (2:389–92). Her description of this project merges into an extended defense of Comte's positivism against his numerous English critics. It is interesting, given Martineau's tendency to rely on her own arguments rather than quote from authorities, that the largest portion of this defense is a quotation from a letter written by her friend Atkinson on the subject of "what Man 'can know'" (2:397–404).

This brings the reader to another work that figures very prominently in the final period of Martineau's autobiography. In spite of Martineau's emphasis, throughout the autobiography, on the responsibility and the integrity of the *individual* author and on writing as a solitary activity, it is *Letters on the Laws of Man's Nature and Development* (1851), of which she is second author after Atkinson, that receives more attention than any other single work. The publication of this book, which ridicules all religious thought, brought about a permanent breach with her once beloved brother and closest childhood companion James, an eminent Unitarian minister. Martineau credits Atkinson for developing her courage to speak her true convictions, regardless of the consequences in her personal or public life (2:370). However, it seems to have been Martineau, not the more reluctant Atkinson, who instigated the publication of the letters (2:336). Martineau not only comments on the beauty of Atkinson's style (most of the letters are his) but refers to him as "the only person, of the multitude I have known, who has clearly apprehended [the] central truth" that science is "the sole and eternal basis of wisdom" (2:332). Furthermore,

> I have found Mr. Atkinson's knowledge of Man, general and particular, physical, intellectual and moral, theoretical and practical, greater than I ever met with elsewhere, in books or conversation; and I immediately discovered that his superior knowledge was due to his higher and truer point of view, whereby he could cast light from every part of the universe upon the organisation and action of Man, and use and test the analogies from without in their application to the world within. (2:335)

Martineau's glowing assessment of Atkinson seems inconsistent with his public reputation, either then or now. Such extravagant language calls to mind Mill's treatment of his wife in his autobiography. Like Mill, Martineau seems to translate personal affection into intellectual praise. At any rate, Martineau's relationship with Atkinson is closely connected to her relative happiness and intellectual equilibrium in her final period. Martineau's description of her life at the lakes is also marked by her series of public lectures (2:301–2), her experiments in farming (2:340), and, in general, more social interaction than at any previous period, though her life is still dominated by writing and publication. In fact it is only during this period that she obtains a real desk and quill pens in place of her old steel one (2:411). The one great writing project that comes toward the end of Martineau's narrative is the writing of leaders for the *Daily News*. After 1852, this kind of journalism becomes her chief activity, an activity, though Martineau did not know when she wrote of it, which would dominate the remaining twenty-one years of her life not covered by the autobiography.

Martineau's final "incident" to relate is the heart problem responsible for her supposed "fatal" illness, in process as she writes the autobiography. She closes with an Augustinian coda, a recapitulation of her philosophy of life that emphasizes her perfect reconciliation with death. Free from all religious superstitions, she can contemplate eternity with peace of mind: "if the universe be full of life, I cannot see how it can signify whether the one human faculty of consciousness of identity be preserved and carried forward, when all the rest of the organisation is gone to dust" (2:439). She goes on to offer a prophetic, meliorist vision of the future, reaffirming the "great law" of "Progress" (2:447) and notes with satisfaction that religious institutions are vanishing (2:458–61).

Thus Martineau's narrative of personal development is embedded in history, in an "age of transition," just as surely as is Mill's, and, like Mill's, it implies a Comtean, positivistic interpretation of history. Like both Newman and Mill, Martineau as narrator is extremely sensitive to her controversial public reputation, careful to outline her influences, both through reading and through personal contact, careful to describe her opinions and philosophy of life at the various stages of her development—always in terms of the mature position at which she will eventually arrive in her narrative. And each successive publication—including *Society in America* and even *Life in the Sick-Room*—no matter how successful monetarily, is judged deficient or flawed insofar as it still carries remnants of her old "metaphysical" philosophy of life, though Martineau obviously treasures each publication for its own sake. As each successive intellectual influence is outgrown and found inadequate—Unitarianism, the Whig program for political reform—it is cast aside and criticized by Martineau with very little allowance for nostalgia. As in the case of Mill, her whole life is an education. Like Owen with his spiritualism, Martineau is somewhat defensive about her "final" commitment to mesmerism, if not to her philosophical atheism as a whole, but unlike Owen, she deals directly with the subject. To an even greater extent than Mill, and much like Trollope, Spencer, and Darwin, she defines her life in terms of her publications. Like most Victorian autobiographers, she is careful to give her account of public controversies (and in her case there are many) and justify her actions as far as possible.

Martineau is the ultimate producer of literary texts. Writing and publishing constitutes her work, her duty in life, and she pursues this work and duty with the fullest possible, eminently Victorian engagement. Her work is drudgery and yet she cheerfully commits herself to it. Only the equally prolific Spencer will include more details about his books and articles. As with Mill (and with several others, as we will see), her compulsive behavior as described in the text is clearly linked to illness and disability, and illness and disability in turn liberate her from social responsibilities, ironically freeing her for more of the only work that matters: thinking and the production of texts. As we have seen, the autobiographical genre tends to squeeze out other functions from the narrative in the text, until primarily the production of (itself and other) texts and activities closely related to their production carry forward the plot.

Like Owen, Martineau includes many details from her childhood, but in her case there is no idyll to describe. Her youth is one of anxiety, painful self-consciousness, loneliness, illness. The "springtime" of her life does not come until middle age. The spirit of courage and defiance in young Martineau's determined effort to create a literary career for herself and the deafness that becomes symbolic of her isolation are appropriate to Martineau's overriding individualistic, laissez-faire model of human experience, but these factors do not altogether obscure the educational opportunities provided by her parents or the network of family members and friends of the family who support her in various ways. The very fact that the autobiography was published together with the "memorials" of her close friend and admirer Maria Weston Chapman reminds the reader that Martineau is not wholly isolated from close personal contacts and associations. Nevertheless, Martineau's story is of an *individual* in a hard if not altogether hostile world and, in particular, of a fearless individual consciousness linked to certain public works, that is, publications that will presumably live on after her death.

One obvious question to ask is whether Martineau's story about herself differs significantly from those of the men who published autobiographies both before and after she did. Of course, there are some distinctive features related to Martineau's gender. Particularly in the first two periods of the autobiography, she makes poignant references to conventional women's work and women's place in the home as she describes her self-formation as a thinker and writer. There are relatively more references to family members and family concerns, and her role as a caregiver to her aged mother and aunt reinforces her feminine persona. Throughout the text she gives advice to aspiring writers, as many autobiographers do, but Martineau most often directs this advice specifically to young women who may follow in her footsteps. Overall, Martineau implies that it is especially difficult for a female writer to establish herself, but that her own life proves that it can be done, and that it is in the realm of science that women are given the best chance to be successful. Her best-known comment on the "Woman Question" in the autobiography concerns the issue of education:

> [W]omen, like men, can obtain whatever they show themselves fit for. Let them be educated,—let their powers be cultivated to the extent for which the means are already provided, and all that is wanted or ought to be desired will follow of course. Whatever a woman proves herself able to do, society will be thankful to see her do,—just as if she were a man. (1:401)

Her attitudes toward the roles of wife and mother are not particularly unconventional, though she is fearless in attacking conventional ideas in other areas. She reserves her rhetoric of controversy for human, not gender issues.

Although Martineau defines herself as a woman with some special women's concerns, I have argued that her autobiography is typical of the genre as defined here, however male dominated that genre might have been in nineteenth-century England. Linda H. Peterson has argued that Martineau's use of "gossip" in the long, previously published insert on "literary lionism" in period 4 of the autobiography is evidence of feminine discourse that "irrupts" in the otherwise masculine, logocentric discourse she has imposed upon herself.[12] Supposedly the fact that Martineau interrupts her Comtean narrative of intellectual growth to tell anecdotes about vain writers makes her text more feminine. It seems to me, however, that Martineau's section on literary lionism is more properly seen as evidence of the impurity of autobiographical discourse. It is not at all unusual for autobiographers to juxtapose memoirs or reminiscences with narratives of intellectual development, as is seen throughout this study. Even Darwin, in his slender volume, finds space to gossip about fellow scientists and celebrities he met in London.

It may very well be, however, that part of Martineau's strategy here is to show that male writers can be just as vain as female writers.[13] Martineau seems painfully conscious of the problematics involved in the relationship between writer and reader, and she is intent on showing her absolute integrity as an author, especially because she is a woman. Martineau wants to believe that her works are significant because they are aligned with the inexorable laws that are shaping human history.

Chapter 5

Anthony Trollope, *An Autobiography* (1883)

Trollope's is the best-known autobiography written by a nineteenth-century British novelist.[1] Its reputation, however, is based on striking qualities that some readers have seen as negative, especially Trollope's refusal to attempt to probe into his writer's imagination or analyze the creative process in more than a superficial way. The most notorious passages, of course, are concerned with Trollope's description of his own writing system, with its precise quotas of words and pages, his close accounting of money received for each manuscript, and his insistence upon treating novel writing as a trade like any other, comparing himself and his novels to a cobbler and his shoes. The *Autobiography* seems to portray the creative artist as Philistine. Nevertheless, Trollope's recent biographers claim that the "disclosures" of the autobiography were already generally known to contemporary readers and that the book did not really retard Trollope's posthumous reputation.[2]

The book treats Trollope's entire "life and career" and was written during the period 1875-76,[3] less than a decade before the novelist's death at the end of 1882. Entrusting it to his son Henry for editing, Trollope wanted the work to be posthumous, and he adopts the voice of one who speaks from beyond the grave.

It might be expected that the most prolific Victorian storyteller would be especially sensitive to the problematic qualities of the genre, which relate both to "story" and "character." Trollope acknowledges his consciousness of them at once by giving a very restrictive description of what he might accomplish in what he calls, "for the want of a better name," his autobiography.

> It will not be so much my intention to speak of the little details of my private life, as of what I, and perhaps others around me,

have done in literature; of my failures and successes ... and of the opening which a literary career offers to men and women for the earning of their bread. (1)

The "garrulity of old age" and the necessity of narrative form will cause him to "say something of myself," and yet "that I, or any man, should tell everything of himself, I hold to be impossible" (1). Furthermore, he ends his book with another statement that blatantly denies to the autobiography just the inner narrative of selfhood that many critics and scholars have found most interesting about the genre.

> It will not, I trust, be supposed by any reader that I have intended in this so-called autobiography to give a record of my inner life. No man ever did so truly,—and no man ever will. Rousseau probably attempted it, but who doubts but that Rousseau has confessed in much the thoughts and convictions rather than the facts of his life? (365)

Trollope thus denies to the *Autobiography* the level of characterization that one might expect to find in one of his novels. It is worthwhile to reproduce these lengthy quotations, even though they have been cited frequently by scholars, because they make explicit assumptions about the genre and its conventions that are implicit or only partially articulated in many other Victorian autobiographies.

Nevertheless, though Trollope's *Autobiography* is largely a memoir, as he frequently calls it in his text, and though it is replete with shop talk that is at least ostensibly directed toward the budding novelist, it has a very clearly delineated plot line based on the author's self-development.

In the most obvious sense, the narrative is a tale of worldly success. As every competent novelist knows, such a story must begin low in order to make the eventual heights significant. Trollope's first-person account of childhood and early adulthood is among the most pathetic (and self-pitying) in Victorian letters,[4] challenging Dickens's fictionalized account in *David Copperfield*. The chronicle of misery and frustration in the first chapter, "My Education, 1815 to 1834," is continued in the third chapter's account of his unhappy years in London's "General Post Office, 1834–1841." The chronological account is interrupted by chapter 2, the story of his remarkable mother who, in her fifties, after a life of relative idleness, rescued her ineffectual, consumptive husband and sick children from abject poverty by writing, first, a book on America, and then a long series of novels.

At school, the poor and awkward Trollope was ostracized by the other boys and unjustly flogged by the teachers, while he learned nothing, even within the limited classical curriculum. At home he lived in a dirty, dilapidated farmhouse with his tragically unsuccessful father and later with his entire family in exile from his father's creditors in Belgium. Although he found some direction in life when he was appointed to a clerkship in the London Post Office in 1834, his seven-year tenure there was characterized by wasted time, continued debt, and unappreciative superiors.

In short, the first twenty-six years of his life were "years of suffering, disgrace, and inward remorse" (60). The event that transformed his life was his post office appointment as a surveyor's clerk in Ireland. "This was the first good fortune of my life" (59). There is no doubt about the status of this turning point in his life story: "From the day on which I set my foot in Ireland all these evils went away from me. Since that time who has had a happier life than mine?" (60). In this tale of material success and well-being, Trollope's move to Ireland is structurally equivalent to a religious conversion in a spiritual autobiography.

The title of the fourth chapter, "Ireland—My First Two Novels" signals the most important single aspect of the Irish transition. In his new, happier position, Trollope was able to muster the energy and determination to begin, very slowly and initially with meager results, his second, and ultimately major, profession of writing novels. During this period, he also met and married Rose Heseltine and began to engage in the sport of fox hunting, which was to become almost an obsession with him, up until the present time of the autobiography.

Beginning with chapter 4, a bit less than one-quarter through the book, nearly all of the twenty chapter titles refer to novels or novel writing: from "Ireland—My First Two Novels, 1841–1848" to *"The Way We Live Now and The Prime Minister."* The one exception is chapter 16, where "Beverly" refers, not to a novel, but to the borough where Trollope stood for election in an unsuccessful attempt to sit in Parliament in 1868.

Trollope's *Autobiography* offers an extreme example of a common element of Victorian autobiographies already discussed in previous chapters: the history of his publications. Newman's letters and essays reflect his evolving religious positions as he moves toward his final stance. In similar fashion, Mill's works demonstrate his opinions at each successive stage of mental growth, though his works tend to have less of a documentary function and more of an autonomous status. To a large extent they incorporate Mill's thought and the meaning of his life insofar as the public is concerned. The same could be said about Martineau's treatment of her publications. In Trollope's case, his novels and other publications are not presented as illustrating an evolving consciousness or theory of life. They do illustrate an increasing novelistic skill, but the novels seem to be important primarily because they demonstrate Trollope's increasing financial success as well as his social status as a novelist.

Although these works of art do not represent a meaningful evolution of thought or central theory of life, they do represent a shared imaginary world between writer and audience. And in fact there is a certain development within his imaginary world, as sets of characters grow and change from novel to novel in the Barsetshire series, and especially in the Palliser series, which contains Trollope's beloved Plantagenet Palliser and Lady Glencora, his favorite characters and in his opinion the principal basis of his reputation: "I do not think it probable that my name will remain among those who in the next century will be known as writers of English prose fiction; but if it does, that permanence of success will probably rest on the characters of Plantagenet Palliser, Lady Glencora, and the Rev. Mr. Crawley" (361). Trollope says he does not expect his readers to share his joyful awareness of his characters' development through novels published years apart, but he is implicitly urging his readers to reread a group of his works as a roman-fleuve.

It is Trollope's developing success as a novelist, however, and not the development of fictional characters that provides the main story line beginning with his life in Ireland. From that point on, Trollope's continuing career with the post office provides an important subplot. To a certain extent, Trollope's position as postal official is analogous to that of Mill with the East India Company because it provides him with a base of financial support and the opportunity to write. Unlike Mill's position, however, Trollope's post office career continues to be an important part of his personal identity and a source of pride, and the development of this career is reported along with that of the artistic one. Trollope makes a point of his ability to continue to devote himself to his post office career and maintain his integrity as "a thoroughly efficient public servant" (133) even after his novelistic career has moved ahead.

Following Trollope's move to Ireland, the great turning point of his life, events that serve as important plot functions in Trollope's narrative are the publication of his first novel, *The Macdermots of Ballycloran* (1847); the publication of his first successful novels, *The Warden* (1855) and *Barchester Towers* (1857); his return to England and subsequent association with the *Cornhill Magazine* (1859–60); the attainment of his object of "a position among literary men" and "an income on which I might live in ease and comfort" (167) in 1862; and his resignation from the post office to support himself and his family entirely from his earnings as a writer in 1867.

His goal from the beginning of his novelistic career had been "to make an income on which I and those belonging to me might live in comfort" (108). Appropriately enough, in his final chapter Trollope reproduces a chronological list of his nearly fifty novels and other publications, each entry complete with "total sums received" and the grand total of nearly £69,000 that represented his lifelong earnings as a writer (363–64). Finally, the story of his life is literally summed up by a list of books and income. And although he does not claim to be the finest English novelist, he does claim to be the most prolific:

> And so I end the record of my literary performances,—which I think are more in amount than the works of any other living English author. If any English authors not living have written more—as may probably have been the case—I do not know who they are. (362)

Several observations may be made about the narrative structure of Trollope's *Autobiography*. As already noted, Trollope most emphatically declares that his narrative is not that of an inner or even of a private life. When he briefly mentions his marriage on 11 June 1844, and remarks that "perhaps I ought to name that happy day as the commencement of my better life, rather than the day on which I first landed in Ireland" (68), the remark has the effect of lighthearted gallantry. Trollope's relationship with his wife is not part of the story he has to tell; after all, "My marriage was like the marriage of other people, and of no special interest to any one except my wife and me" (71). In the tradition of Gibbon, Trollope follows the traditional life-and-career format, and to a certain extent, of course, the *Autobiography* is the portrait of an artist, or rather an account of his development into a mature artist, but not nearly to the extent that one might expect in a writer's self-history. Trollope does at least mention his early reading of literature and the habit of daydreaming or "castle building" that later grew into the creation of an imaginary world peopled by his fictional characters. He analyzes his early attempts at fiction writing and compares them to what he was able to accomplish later. However, he foregrounds the development of increasing commercial success. Though he does evaluate most of his novels as to their effectiveness of characterization and plot, there is not a strong sense of developing artistry. Nevertheless, certain insights into the character of Trollope the protagonist are related to the structure of the narrative.

Most important are those concerning the descriptions of his favorite pastime of hunting, that is, of riding to hounds, which he adopted soon after arriving in Ireland. "It will, I think, be accorded to me by Essex men generally that I have ridden hard. The cause of my delight in the amusement I have never been able to analyse to my own satisfaction" (171). It seems obvious, first, that Trollope's acknowledged need for the esteem of his fellow man and for acceptance by important and influential people of the higher classes, a need to which he refers several times in the book, is satisfied to some extent by this patrician yet rousing sport, but the act of riding itself becomes a metaphor for Trollope's life. In describing his apparently irrational desire for riding (he is overweight and awkward, with very poor eyesight) Trollope seems to be conscious of its metaphoric appropriateness. In referring to his current (book time) resolution to give up his horses at last, he says, "I think that I may say with truth that I rode hard to the very end" (352). Trollope's compulsive, energetic riding represents the way he has led his life, that is, the way it is represented in the narrative of his autobiography. Trollope accomplished his goals in life, most particularly success as an extremely prolific novelist, by behavior that can also be termed compulsive and energetic. Of course, his ill-conceived, unsuccessful attempt to sit in

Parliament, at least partially inspired by his desire to defy the advice of a deceased uncle, is also an example. Thus, Trollope's *Autobiography* is the story of a man riding hard.

In addition, it may be noted that the narrative line of increasing success after a decisive turning point is consistent with the meliorist vision of life Trollope expresses in outlining his political position as a "conservative liberal," a position which he says never changed during his lifetime (291). Unlike the previously discussed autobiographies, however, Trollope's narrative does not lead up to (or promise) a controlling idea or philosophy of life that serves to define selfhood—it does lead up to a collection of novels, some of which may live for a time in the public imagination.

Trollope's autobiography, although it certainly does not read like one of his novels, does contain isolated scenes with dramatic and, most often, comic effects. The scenes in which Trollope unintentionally douses with ink his despotic post office superior Colonel Maberly (who had been falsely accusing him of theft) (47), is embarrassed in his office by a lady accusing him of falsely promising to marry her daughter (47–48), makes a furious pitch for his new novel to the publisher Edward Chapman while Chapman holds a poker in his hand (117), and is refused hospitality by a brusque Brigham Young during an American visit (350) are examples (the self-irony really showing the protagonist to advantage).

These scenes, unlike Owen's loosely connected anecdotes, do not seriously impede the flow of the narrative, nor do Trollope's relatively brief reminiscences of people he has known. However, Trollope does interrupt the narrative of his self-history to deliver lengthy advice and opinions on the subject of novels and novel writing, which after all he has announced to be the main purpose of his autobiography. As might be expected, Trollope reserves the bulk of this discourse until the point in the narrative when his protagonist has attained the status of a successful novelist, after he has become or nearly become Trollope the author-narrator. He does not wait for a final philosophical chapter, however. As already noted, he interrupts his narrative to devote three whole chapters (12–15) to this discourse before returning to the story of his late career (the period beginning with his resignation from the post office). Trollope is not as self-indulgent as many other Victorian autobiographers in quoting himself, but he does insert a long quotation from his preface to the

Vicar of Bullhampton ("I wish to have it read"), which argues for his moral purpose in telling his story of a fallen woman (329–32). In this he joins generations of novelists who have made similar claims.

The rhetorical stance of Trollope's narrator can be described as frank and forthright. Although he talks a great deal about his novels and may be said to boast about his enormous production and his stamina in holding two careers, he is careful not to overestimate his own status as a novelist—for example, the public would accept posthumous novels from Dickens but probably not from him, and readers in the next century will probably not remember his novels (346). He admiringly describes his mother's literary feats but does not exaggerate the merits of her novels. He is critical of Thackeray's excessive use of satire, though he acknowledges him to be the first English novelist of his time. He does not withhold his negative opinions even about prominent people (especially his novelist peers and his superiors in the post office). Sir Rowland Hill, in spite of his leading role in establishing the penny post, is ignorant of human nature. Although Dickens is the most popular English novelist, none of his characters are human beings (248).

Trollope the author-narrator has plenty of opinions about the post office and civil service in general—merit exams are no good, for example—but of course his opinions about novelists and novel writing are the most significant ones. Addressing himself to the aspiring novelist—"Oh, my young aspirant" (211)—his primary position is that novel writing is a trade. In this Trollope is much like Martineau.

With this pragmatic view of the profession in mind, and despite what "the critics" will say, he advises regular working hours and rapid writing. Implicit throughout the "handbook" sections of the autobiography is the idea of Trollope as model writer—advice from the master. In fact, those passages expressly directed to young writers are fairly brief. For the most part, Trollope, like most other autobiographers, is primarily defending his practices and views to the public rather than offering advice to others. The genre allows him to set the record straight concerning his own novels by giving the author's own assessment of each (the *Last Chronicle of Barset* is the overall best), condemn the superficiality and dishonesty of modern criticism, explain his own critical position that delineation of character precedes plot, defend the social importance and didactic function of fiction (the author as moralist or even "preacher"), and rank his fellow English novelists and their works in order of their greatness (*Henry Esmond* is the greatest novel). Using the license of the autobiographer, Trollope mines his long planned but never completed "History of English Prose Fiction" (215) for this discourse.

The narrator's overall frankness or even bluntness seems to be characteristic of the historical Trollope, who was an outspoken critic of post office procedures, but within the *Autobiography* it is also rhetorically countenanced by his posthumous position—speaking *ex morte*. More specifically, Trollope occasionally uses the posthumous stance to indirectly address particular people. This device of speaking to a specialized audience, even an individual, within the implied audience of the reading public, is especially characteristic of the genre of autobiography and helps to account for its elusive, problematical nature. Often it is a matter of addressing one's children, as in Darwin's autobiography, to be discussed in chapter 7.

The most striking example from Trollope's book is his affectionate praise of John Everett Millais. "These words, should he ever see them, will tell him of my regard—as one living man never tells another" (150). On the other hand, Trollope's references to his sons in the autobiography are somewhat condescending. Overall, Trollope's ostensible rhetorical strategy is to satisfy public curiosity about his novelistic career.

In spite of Trollope's rhetorical frankness and his seemingly scrupulously objective evaluation of his own works and that of others, certain characteristics of the *Autobiography* have invited readers to look beneath the surface of the text.[5] Most importantly, Trollope's evaluation of his "miserable" youth is difficult to accept at face value. "My boyhood was, I think, as unhappy as that of a young gentleman could well be" (2) and "I have been flogged oftener than any human being alive" (18) are typical comments. Of course, it can be argued that Trollope's feelings of bitterness, resentment, and self-pity are quite genuine and that his extravagant statements are true *to him*. His contempt for the "lily-livered curs" in school at Sunbury who allowed him to be unjustly and severely punished by the headmaster for infractions he knew nothing about is forcefully expressed: "I remember their names well, and almost wish to write them here" (6). As a young adult, his unjust treatment at the hands of his superior, Sir Francis Freeling, in the post office is also expressed with conviction: "I can remember well the keenness of my anguish when I was treated as though I were unfit for any useful work" (44). However, Trollope's shaping of experience in his narrative to create a totally miserable life before the happy turning point of his Irish appointment does seem extravagant; after all, Trollope apparently made lifelong friends during his Harrow days, though he writes of that time as though he were universally hated, so that "something of the disgrace of my school-days have clung to me all through life" (17). The disjunction between the pre-Ireland and post-Ireland Trollope is an important aspect of the relationship between the present time of Trollope's *Autobiography* and the past time of the narrative. In retrospection, before the great turning point, past time is more mythic, with well-defined, although negative, meanings. Afterward, the happy part of his life is more "realistically" portrayed. Trollope does not stress the distancing, or distorting, effects of memory. When he mentions memory loss, it is most often in regard to the details of his less important books. His favorite novels, on the other hand, are very clear in his mind, and he continues to "live with" his most cherished characters. There is relatively little tension between memory and documentation of historical facts in Trollope's book because the foregrounded history of his publications is unambiguous and he has kept an accounting of his income from books. As already noted, the list of publications and earnings given in Trollope's last chapter to a large extent sums up the meaning of his life as presented in the book.

An especially intriguing aspect of the relationship between selfhood and environment is seen in the role of Trollope's mother. Obviously, Victorian autobiography is full of powerful fathers. Although sometimes interpreted as oppressors of their sons, their roles in the self-histories of the sons are usually very complex and often ambivalent. James Mill and Robert Owen not only educate their sons according to their own schemes but provide a start in life for them along the lines of their own careers by locating a job in the East India Company in one case and offering a mission to an experimental community in the other. More subtly, the elder Mill and Owen provide role models for their sons that help them to define their life goals, however much they may diverge from the opinions and beliefs of their fathers as their own mature. The term *role model*, however, is inadequate to express the dominant *presence* of such a figure in the boy's life.

In Trollope's case, the mother occupied an analogous position. Although Trollope does not explicitly attribute his role as novelist to the influence of his mother, his narrative makes this relationship clear. Trollope's regimen of severely disciplined writing during the early morning hours is a more calculated version of his mother's heroic efforts, and even more significantly, he inherits from her the view of novel writing as primarily a craft, a source of income. In her case, novel writing meant economic survival for her and her family. In his, appropriately for the second generation, it represents the additional income and the public esteem that will make him truly successful in life, the key to ultimately relinquishing the outsider's role he had been fated to play in childhood. Even his travel books have their precedent in his mother's famous book about the Americans.

When compared to other autobiographies by Victorian men of letters, Trollope's book contains very little of spiritual, philosophical, or social vision. Trollope's rough-hewn worldview—his pragmatic and meliorist politics, his ideals of integrity, hard work and gentlemanly behavior—does not carry the universal idealism of Mill's progress of mankind, of Newman's Church, of Martineau's necessarianism. Nevertheless, Trollope's autobiography is not without its prophetic element, particularly in its critical evaluations within the British tradition of the novel. Appropriately enough for a writer in the comedy-of-manners tradition, Trollope looks toward the outward rather than the inward aspects of human experience, the culturally specific rather than the universal.

It might be argued, however, that the ideal of the English gentleman so dear to Trollope and incorporated into his favorite character, Plantagenet Palliser, Duke of Omnium, offers a model of moral behavior with an appeal far beyond the provincial or national.[6] In the character of Palliser and his wife, Trollope has delivered his soul (180), and Palliser is "a perfect gentleman. If he be not, than I am unable to describe a gentleman" (361). Although Trollope's vision of the gentleman may seem hopelessly Victorian, the implications of this ideal as an ethical force (though perhaps a doomed one) in the post-Victorian world were to be developed by later English novelists, notably, Ford Maddox Ford in his tetralogy *Parade's End*.

Chapter 6

John Ruskin, *Praeterita* (1885–89)

Ruskin's autobiography ended his career as a writer; the final chapter, "Joanna's Care," was the last piece of prose that he wrote for publication. *Praeterita* (What is past) was issued irregularly in serial publication during the period 1885–89. As is well known, Ruskin struggled with mental illness throughout this period and apparently planned to continue his autobiography beyond the point he had reached when he was forced to stop (xxxiii).[1] Ruskin lived on until 1900, but his literary career was at an end. *Praeterita*, then, is technically a fragment.

Praeterita has a peculiar status among the canonical Victorian autobiographies. Although generally acknowledged as a prose classic, it is often described in negative terms, as a narrative of failure or an expression of stasis and death.[2] It is certainly the case that Ruskin's autobiography seems to undermine some of the conventions of the genre or at least to call attention to many of the problematic features of autobiography that were discussed in the introduction. If one attempted to arrange the works studied in this book in a developmental sequence, *Praeterita* might be placed last because, more than any of the others, it points toward the twentieth-century concepts of the fictive self and the fragmented self. On the most basic level, the issue of truth and fiction (or truth and falsehood) has long been prominent in *Praeterita* scholarship, as scholars have noted discrepancies between events and attitudes recorded in Ruskin's diaries and other documents and the account of them given in the autobiography.[3]

One of the most obvious characteristics of *Praeterita* is its extremely digressive nature. Although the narrative follows a roughly chronological order, reminiscences that leap forward and backward in narrative past time as well as intrusions of narrative discourse that foreground the process of composition in the present time of the book continually interrupt the narrative line so that there is only a vague sense of chronology.

Praeterita is made up of three volumes, the first two of which contain twelve chapters each. The fact that the third volume contains only four reflects the fragmentary nature of the book. The first two chapters are composed of slightly revised passages from Ruskin's series *Fors Clavigera* and had been previously published during the period 1871–75. "The Springs of Wandel" covers roughly the years from Ruskin's birth in 1819 to his fifth year, in 1824, while "Herne-Hill Almond Blossoms" moves to the year 1826. The two chapters actually give a generalized account of Ruskin's childhood, however, with only an approximate sense of time or chronological order, but they contain numerous individual descriptive scenes and anecdotes.

The third chapter, "The Banks of Tay," begins by reviewing the old *Fors* account of his childhood and continues with anecdotes through 1828. Chapter 4, "Under New Tutorships," which extends to the year 1834, develops more narrative momentum with the notation of developmental events such as Henry Telford's fateful gift of Rogers's *Italy* to the boy Ruskin, his first European tour with his mother and father, his experiences in school.

However, Ruskin introduces chapter 5, "Parnassus and Plymlimmon," with the statement that he has allowed his "boyish achievements and experiments in art to run on to a date much in advance of the early years which were most seriously eventful for me in good and evil" (87), and he backtracks to cover approximately the same period (1829–35), adding various details, including an account of the death of his "Croydon aunt" and a description of her sons.

In chapter 6, "Schaffhausen and Milan," Ruskin pauses to focus on a single year—1833—the year of the Ruskin family's first continental journey. The chapter contains a description of Ruskin's "first sight of the Alps," a foregrounded event that must be seen as a significant turning point in any reading of Ruskin's autobiography as a story of development. Chapter 7, "Papa and Mama," begins by describing the young Ruskin's four "occupations" in 1834—poetry, engraving, architecture, and geology—but, as the title suggests, turns to a lengthy discussion of his parents. Chapters 8, "Vester, Camenae," and 9, "The Col de la Faucille," are set in the year 1835 and cover influences on Ruskin's writing style (especially that of Byron) and the lasting effect of French and Swiss architecture and landscape as seen in that year.

Chapter 10, "Quem Tu, Melpomene," is concerned with the year 1836 and is notable for its treatment of his infatuation with Adèle Domecq and his entry into Oxford, while chapter 11 focuses on Oxford experiences and treats primarily the year 1837. Chapter 12, "Roslyn Chapel," extends Ruskin's self-history to the year 1839 and describes the beginning of his writing career: his heated reply to the criticism of Turner in *Blackwoods* and his article "The Poetry of Architecture."

Ruskin begins his second volume with the prediction that it must be "less pleasing to the general reader" because he must "talk ... more of myself. For as I look deeper into the mirror, I find myself a more curious person than I had thought" (243). However, no new line of intensive introspection is introduced, and Ruskin's digressive style continues to blunt the narrative force of such developmental events as the epiphany during his drawing of the ivy at Norwood (311) in chapter 4, "Fontainebleau." Increasingly, Ruskin documents his first impressions of various scenes by quoting from his diary of the time. Chapters 8–10 contain a somewhat sketchy account of the composition and reception of the first two volumes of Ruskin's first major work, *Modern Painters*, in the years 1843–46.

By chapter 11, "L'Hôtel du Mont Blanc," Ruskin has worked his way up to 1849, and the age of thirty. Ironically, as he reaches the point at which his "true work" begins, "for what it is worth" (437)—evidently alluding to the new social consciousness that would lead him to a new kind of thought and experience—his "days of youthful happiness" are closed, and thus his narrative, chiefly based as it is on "pleasurable" memories associated with landscape, has little momentum. The final chapter of volume 2, "Otterburn," is especially digressive in its description of personal friendships and Scottish scenery and character and does nothing to advance the chronology of Ruskin's self-history.

Even considering Ruskin's digressive style from the beginning of *Praeterita*, the closing chapters of volume 2 show a decreasing coherence. However, in chapter 1 of volume 3, "The Grande Chartreuse," it is as though Ruskin makes one last effort to control his material and forge it into narrative form, going so far as to outline the "main facts" of the years 1850–60, though they were "for the most part wasted in useless work" (483). He also seems to be building toward an essential turning point in his life, his final break with his Puritan faith, but, as will be discussed below, this crisis finally does not occupy the expected position in his story. After the anticlimactic close of this chapter, the narrative line in the final three chapters again proceeds by loosely connected anecdotal material—with only nostalgic references to the tragic affair with Rose La Touche—concluding with the barely coherent but occasionally poetic chapter entitled "Joanna's Care," and coming to rest with one of the most striking passages of the book, one that is worth examining in some detail.

Ruskin leads into his last paragraph with reminiscences of "Elysian" walks with "Joanie" (Joan Severn) and "Paradisiacal" walks with "Rosie" (Rose La Touche) at his home twenty years before, "under the peach blossom branches by the little glittering stream which I have paved with crystal for them" (560). He remarks that the waters of this "tiny river" were "sweeter to my thirst than the fountains of Trevi or Branda." This association leads him in the final paragraph to think back to the last time he saw both of these famous fountains.

The last time he saw the Trevi was from the window of Joseph Severn's (Joanna's father-in-law's) house in 1872. The old man was painting a picture of the Marriage in Cana "and delighted himself by painting the crystal and ruby glittering of the changing rivulet of water out of the Greek vase, glowing into wine." Then Ruskin recalls seeing Fonte Branda in Siena with Charles Norton, the man who had urged Ruskin to write *Praeterita* and thus an appropriate companion in this final scene.

> We drank of it together, and walked together that evening on the hills above, where the fireflies among the scented thickets shone fitfully in the still undarkened air. *How* they shone! moving like fine-broken starlight through the purple leaves. How they shone! through the sunset that faded into thunderous night as I entered Siena three days before, the white edges of the mountainous clouds still lighted from the west, and the openly golden sky calm behind the Gate of Siena's heart, with its still golden words, "Cor magis tibi Sena pandit," and the fireflies every-

where in sky and cloud rising and falling, mixed with the lightning, and more intense than the stars. (562)

The method of composition that governs Ruskin's final passage is that used throughout the book, but the process of association is accelerated so that it is barely coherent. The image of the tiny "glittering stream" is associated with the two fountains but is actually first connected with the image of the "glittering of the changing rivulet of water" in Severn's painting, which is connected again, not to the fountain itself, but to the shining fireflies, which in turn suggest "fine-broken starlight," which is contrasted to the "openly golden sky," which is compared to the "golden" words on the city gate, an image followed by the fireflies once again, now mixed with lightning and compared to the stars.

Only the connected light imagery holds the reminiscences together. "How things bind and blend themselves together!" exclaims Ruskin at the beginning of the last paragraph. Time and distance mean nothing in the present memory of these images.

There are some problems with the grammar and coherence of the passage. After the second incantation of "How they shone!" the preposition "through" is ambiguous because the phrase that it initiates refers to a time three days prior to the time of the evening scene shared with Norton, when Ruskin rode into the city and read the inscription on the city gates. But with the conjunction "and" the sentence again turns to the subject of the fireflies, and what is the time here? Most probably it is three days before, when he had first seen the fireflies, perhaps against the background of an approaching storm in the distance, "mixed with the lightning," but the question is really irrelevant. The scene three days before and the one shared with Norton have become one because they exist simultaneously in Ruskin's memory. The symbolic value of the scene as connected with Norton's friendship provides part of the deeply moving effect of this passage. If this stream-of-consciousness conclusion suggests Ruskin's approaching madness, it also illustrates his genius.

Although Ruskin creates an intimately personal world, it is an external world that revolves around a sensitive observer rather than the inner world of a self-directed mind: the reader sees what Ruskin regards to be crucial points in the development of his mind, usually associated with specific visual images, but these points do not form a single, unified thread of self-development, nor are they related with a sense of intensity. Unencumbered by intense self-analysis (rhetorically, at least), Ruskin *assumes* a synthesis of the feelings characteristic of a healthy aesthetic life, but it is the product of a gradual, natural unfolding of sensibility. In fact, he foregrounds the formulaic transitions that would signal the passage from one stage to another and subtly plays with reader expectation regarding the conventions of autobiography.

Ruskin repeatedly calls attention to the distinction between his present self and his present act of writing the book and his past self and his past actions and reactions. Ultimately, this discrepancy is resolved through a method resembling—and no doubt influenced by—Wordsworth's use of "spots of time" in his *Prelude*.[4] Through Ruskin's evocation of the old sights, chosen moments of past time exist within the present time of the book—but Ruskin does not attempt to conceal the artifice by which one becomes the other. The reader is continually reminded of the shaping process. Ruskin frequently refers to patterns or stages in his life, but he usually does so in a casual manner that suggests that such shaping schemes are somewhat arbitrary and not to be taken entirely seriously. After all, his explicitly impressionistic method allows him to record events as they occur to the author-narrator; consequently, his life story lacks the ostensible unity and coherence that would have been imposed by a more detailed outline or plan for the book. He writes, "I think my history will, in the end be completest if I write as its connected subjects occur to me, and not with a formal chronology of plan" (128). While Ruskin refuses to reduce his life to a single strand, however, he attempts to identify as many strands as he can. He writes,

> Whether in the biography of a nation or of a single person, it is alike impossible to trace it steadily through successive years. Some forces are falling while others strengthen, and most act irregularly, or else at uncorresponding periods of renewed enthusiasm after intervals of lassitude. For all clearness of exposition, it is necessary to follow first one, then another, without confusing notices of what is happening in other directions. (169)

Because Ruskin does not attempt to reconstruct a strong sense of a single, unified life process, *Praeterita* lacks a strong temporal movement.[5] Although Ruskin in general moves forward in time from one chapter to another, he skips backward and forward so that there is little consistent forward momentum.

One game concerning the protagonist's development that Ruskin as narrator plays with the reader is "what might have been" or "if only." He develops this motif in a whimsical and drily humorous manner. If only his parents had given him a Welsh pony and left him in charge of a Welsh guide, "they would have made a man of me there and then... and probably the first geologist of my time in Europe. If only! But they could no more have done it than thrown me... into the Croydon Canal" (96). If his father and mother had kept their youthful guest Charlotte Withers "a month longer, we should have fallen quite melodiously and quietly in love; and they might have given me an excellently pleasant little wife, and set me up, geology and all, in the coal business, without any resistance or farther trouble on my part" (222). In a similar whimsical tone, he describes his early failure to draw the architecture of Rome: "I might have made the most precious records of all the cities in Italy. But all my chances of being anything but what I am were thrown away, or broken short, one after another" (227). And if only Turner had "asked me to come and see him the next day! shown me a pencil sketch, and let me see him lay a wash! He would have saved me ten years of life!" (306). Later, he makes a more serious lament, that he had not been able to maintain the thrill of conscious happiness that he felt in France in 1845: "Another 'had been' this, the gravest of all I lost, the last with which I shall trouble the reader" (378). However, only a few pages later, he writes of the unrealized talents of the architect Edmund Oldfield: "If only—I may still sometimes indulge in a 'might have been' for my friends" (384). It seems to me that Ruskin as author-narrator is self-consciously playful here, a quality that prevents the narrative from degenerating into pathetic self-pity.

Another, more serious, game in which Ruskin indulges, related to what might have been, is that of locating turning points in his life. He locates "four distinct directions" in his youthful work of 1834, "in any one of which my strength might at that time have been fixed by definite encouragement": "the effort to express sentiment in rhyme," "the real love of engraving," "the violent instinct for architecture," and the "geological instinct." He then goes on to explain how the "peculiar character and genius" of his parents influenced his inclinations (120–21). Most of the turning points in his life, however, are associated with places—cities and mountains—rather than with people. Speaking of the first sight of the towers of Abbeville in 1835, he says, "I scarcely know how far I can make even the most sympathetic reader understand their power over my own life" (153).

It turns out that the discovery of Abbeville was the preface to the discovery of Rouen, which along with Geneva and Pisa became one of the "three centres of my life's thought." Mountains are no less prominent: "Both mountains have had enormous influence on my whole life;—the Dole continually and calmly, the Righi at sorrowful intervals, as will be seen. But the Col de la Faucille, on that day of 1835, opened in me in distinct vision the Holy Land of my future work and true home in this world" (167). More poignant is a walk with his father in 1849, which "virtually closed the days of youthful happiness, and began my true work in the world—for what it is worth" (437). But just what Ruskin considers to be his true work is somewhat obscure.

Two turning points that Ruskin biographers inevitably point to are (1) his work in Venice, which led to the publication of *The Stones of Venice* in the early 1850s, where the study of architecture becomes the key to the study of society, and (2) the religious crisis of 1859. Both of these crises he associated, at least in retrospect, with much psychic pain, and to ignore them would be consistent with his pledge to write only about those things that give him pleasure to recall (iii). He does not omit references to them but does not give them the central prominence they would logically assume in a developmental plot of life and career. He makes only passing reference to his career as social and political critic. Deep into the book in volume 2, chapter 9, he remarks upon the degrading way in which the Domecqs viewed their Spanish laborers and French tenantry: this "gave me the first clue to the real sources of wrong in the social laws of modern Europe; and led me necessarily into the political work which has been the most earnest of my life" (409).

The fact is that Ruskin does not locate a dominant, crucial turning point or crisis in his life either in terms of his inner development of mind or in terms of his career as writer-prophet. The closest thing we find in *Praeterita* is chapter 1 of volume 3, "The Grande Chartreuse," which is concerned with his religious crisis. But, as we see when we examine it closely, the series of events does not lead up to the kind of turning point we find in such scenes as Mill's mental crisis.

"The Grande Chartreuse" is the last fully coherent chapter and is, in fact, one of the most carefully organized and least digressive chapters in the book. This is the chapter that briefly treats the years 1850–60, listing a few notable events for each year in outline form. These years, which he calls "for the most part wasted in useless work" (483), saw his major interest shift from art to architecture to society, and the final shift of interest coincided with and was closely related to the loss of his evangelical faith. The chapter certainly deals with the kind of experience that has the potential of generating a total crisis of personality.

The bulk of this chapter is taken up by anecdotes that illustrate in a subtle way Ruskin's religious speculations down through the years that ended in his "unconversion." In 1845, he and his father toured the monastery of the Grande Chartreuse, where he pondered why the monks were blind to the mountain beauty that Ruskin always associated with religion; in 1840, he and his father had toured the Convent of St. Michael, where he had been struck by the hostess-sister's Catholic certainty of salvation; he noticed the beauty of Catholic peasant life in Chamouni in the summers of 1842 and 1844; he admired the monks during his work at Venice but found fault with the Catholic hierarchies; and so on. Ruskin's flirtation with Catholicism is a major theme in the chapter; the culmination is his discovery of an illustrated missal in 1850 or 1851, which "opened new worlds" to him, but he knows that the Catholic faith was simply unavailable to him. Why did he not become a Catholic? "It might as well be asked, why did I not become a fire-worshipper?" (492). Ruskin also records his rejection of "Maurician free-thinking," which he contrasts to an evangelical "seance" that forbade "thinking at all" (489).

The last anecdote in the chapter, however, is the most crucial and well known. One Sunday morning in 1858, Ruskin attended a small Waldensian chapel in the south suburb of Turin. He was struck by the sterility and the narrow-mindedness of the "solitary and clerkless preacher... with a cracked voice" who spoke of the corruption of Turin and the special favor of God enjoyed by the "between nineteen and twenty-four select members of his congregation." Afterward, Ruskin meditated in an art gallery in Turin, looking at Paul Veronese's *Solomon and the Queen of Sheba* and listening to the military music that floated up from the courtyard.

> And as the perfect color and sound gradually asserted their power over me, they seemed finally to fasten me in the old article of Jewish faith, that things done delightfully and rightly, were always done by the help and in the spirit of God. Of course, that hour's meditation in the gallery of Turin only concluded the courses of thoughts which had been leading me to such an end through many years. There was no sudden conversion possible to me, either by preacher, picture, or dulcimer. But that day, my evangelical beliefs were put away, to be debated no more. (495)

The matter ends in quiet rejection. The highly suggestive images of sight and sound in this passage, associated with an artistic sensibility alien to the too-narrow evangelicalism but necessary to a full religious experience, help to define his state of mind but do not anticipate a newly formulated religious or philosophical position to replace the old.

In stark contrast to Martineau and others, Ruskin refers to the evolution of his religious beliefs no more in *Praeterita*. Critics of his work in the 1860s and after find a kind of religion of humanity expressed in his works. And, after 1874, he increasingly turned back to a version of Christianity that restored the piety but not the severe Puritan theology and moralism of his youthful religion. Certainly, references to God and biblical allusions remain central to his work after the "unconversion." But whatever the religious position that Ruskin reached after his rejection of his evangelical heritage, he does not use this reformulation as a centrally important, transcendent affirmation nor even discuss it in his autobiography.

Ruskin implicitly suggests and then deviates from the sort of Romantic pattern used by Mill in his autobiography, and this can be related to his method of composition and mode of consciousness throughout his written works. He did not regard intense self-analysis as the road to truth, and a program such as Mill's deliberate cultivation of the feelings aimed at a new integration of personal faculties was foreign to him. Ruskin, though far from rejecting the importance of human imagination, does tend to reject the independent status of the imagination and stresses the conjunction of human emotions and reality, based on the act of perception. ("The greatest thing a human soul ever does in this world is to *see* something, and tell what it *saw* in a plain way.")[6]

When the reader recalls a major event recorded in *Praeterita*, he or she will almost invariably recall a definite visual image with which it is associated. Most of these major events consist of the act of perception itself, of mountains and cities: "My most intense happinesses have of course been among mountains. But for cheerful, unalloyed, unwearying pleasure, the getting in sight of Abbeville on a fine summer afternoon, jumping out in the courtyard of the Hotel de l'Europe, and rushing down the street to see St. Wulfrun again before the sun was off the towers, are things to cherish the past for,—to the end" (157). There are many "first sights," and the book is, to a large extent, built around them, but perhaps the most memorable is the first sight of the Alps: "They were as clear as crystal, sharp on the pure horizon sky, and already tinged with rose by the sinking sun. Infinitely beyond all that we had ever thought or dreamed. . . . It is not possible to imagine, in any time of the world, a more blessed entrance into life, for a child of such a temperament as mine" (115). The reader gradually realizes that the European scenes described in *Praeterita* lie along a route traversed first by Ruskin and his parents and later by Ruskin alone, again and again through the years: from northern France, south through the Jura Mountains, to Geneva, Switzerland, and on to Mont Blanc, then across the Alps into northern Italy, before returning home by a similar route.[7] This motif of the recurrent journey reinforces the nonprogressiveness of the autobiographical narrative.

Other major events are not directly connected with seeing in a literal sense but nevertheless are associated with prominent visual images. We will recall, for example, Ruskin's contemplation of Paul Veronese's *Solomon and the Queen of Sheba* as he finally lost his old evangelical convictions. But many other "sights" in *Praeterita* become major events, not because they figure heavily in Ruskin's development, but simply because they are incorporated into Ruskin's prose.

One of the most quoted passages in Victorian prose is Ruskin's description of the Rhone, "which flows like one lambent jewel; its surface is nowhere, its ethereal self is everywhere" (326–27).

Two lectures that Ruskin delivered at the London Institution in February 1884, jointly entitled "The Storm-Cloud of the Nineteenth Century," provide a furious, dramatic prelude to the relatively quiet rhetoric of *Praeterita*. It was as though Ruskin's prophetic voice, after thundering its ultimate message, had receded into gentle reflectiveness. To be sure, Ruskin as narrator cannot resist grumbling to his reader about the Crystal Palace (48–49), F. D. Maurice's freethinking theology (488–89), and various other vexations and grievances, but he addresses fewer such targets than do most other Victorian autobiographers, and the great arguments of his later career are conspicuously unemphasized. Of course, Ruskin rhetorically stresses the pleasure of memory, both specific scenes and patterns of images and associations, such as that he links with his Scottish forebears and distinctively Scottish sensibilities. The pain and pathos of loss are at least as prominent as the pleasure of recollection, however. No Victorian autobiographer is more persistent in reinforcing the implied relationship between author-narrator and reader by continual metadiscourse. Ruskin's persona insists on a conversational nearness to the reader. This chattiness and general autobiographicality in reference to personal experiences and personal impressions is a characteristic mode that Ruskin has used throughout his career, but here it is not punctuated by the usual invective. This is formally appropriate in that Ruskin's narrative does not really take its protagonist beyond childhood and the formative years, and thus he never becomes John Ruskin, the mature writer and thinker, who is writing the autobiography.

However, because both the narrative form and rhetoric of the book serve to undercut and deny development, the relationship between narrator and protagonist is, paradoxically, unusually close. The protagonist never grows up, never becomes the author-narrator in the autobiographical narrative, yet at some deep level the narrator is still that same child, adolescent, and young adult because his essential nature is still defined by certain unvarying personal qualities: "patience in looking," "precision of feeling," "analytical power." These static qualities, rather than evolving ideas or a series of publications, are at the heart of the self-identity that binds together narrator and protagonist. To maintain this timeless identity Ruskin must reject the kind of developmental narrative adopted by all of the other autobiographers that we have studied. Ruskin, one of the most prolific Victorian writers, had published about 250 titles in addition to lectures and journal articles, as well as producing an enormous body of personal diaries and correspondence. There is every indication that he was as compulsive, as committed, and as willing to overwork himself in completing his writing projects as was Martineau or any of the other autobiographers. But, unlike the others, he does not really attempt to tell the story of his writing and publishing career.

Just as Ruskin's autobiography represents an extreme in sensibility to the natural world—especially, delight in landscape—it also represents an extreme in elegiac sensibility: melancholy, regret, sorrow over loss. Thus, *Praeterita* is particularly notable for its dialectics between self and environment, the author-narrator and the protagonist, the present time of the book and narrative past time. Ruskin is most adept at recreating or recapturing scenes from his past for the simultaneous entertainment of narrator and implied reader. But since the narrative framework of development is weak and confused, the story cannot remain in the past. The present time, the process of recollection and writing, never far from the awareness evoked by metadiscourse, must become dominant over the story line or plot, and the concomitant shift from past to present time inevitably leads to the elegiac tone.

Ruskin's sharp focus on the act of perception itself foregrounds a relationship between self and environment that goes well beyond the references to natural beauty and nostalgia for home place so common to Victorian autobiographies. Though Ruskin's method is markedly different from those of previous Victorian autobiographers, this method itself implies universal meanings and a prophetic purpose associated with his life history. Thus, largely without the rhetorical discourse of Newman, Mill, or Martineau, Ruskin argues for his vision of the world.

In spite of his impressionistic methodology and love of nature inherited from Romanticism, Ruskin cannot accept the dualism that is inherent in the Romantic epistemological model. Whether the subject and object are fused, or the object is somehow brought into the subject, or the subject is projected into the object, in the creative act, the Romantic model assumes a dualism in subject and object that exists in reality. Further, it is the subject or the self or the ego that acts in any case, and there is a strong tendency inherent in this model to aggrandize the ego.

In the process of writing *Praeterita*, Ruskin increasingly probes into his sense of selfhood and finds himself "more curious" than he had ever supposed. But though he makes this discovery, his emphasis is not on his uniqueness as an individual but on the external world that he had been "reading" and interpreting to the English public throughout his career. Underlying the art and social criticism had always been this central concern, and he turns to it with a final reaffirmation in *Praeterita*. Although Ruskin creates an intimately personal world, it is an external world that revolves around a sensitive observer rather than the inner world of a self-directed mind. Unencumbered by the rhetoric of his recent social criticism, Ruskin's voice retains its central concern with universal truth, the wellspring of its prophetic function.

Chapter 7

Charles Darwin, *Autobiography* (1887)

Darwin wrote the main narrative of his autobiography during the period May–August 1876 and made some additions during the next six years before he died in 1882 at the age of seventy-three. The work was first published, five years after Darwin's death,[1] as part of the *Life and Letters of Charles Darwin* (1887), edited by his son Francis. Various omissions were made in this version of the autobiography, principally due to the sensitivity of Darwin's widow to the skeptical religious beliefs expressed in the original manuscript. In the twentieth century, enlarged versions appeared. Finally, in 1958, his granddaughter, Nora Barlow, edited a version in which all the previous omissions were restored (8).

The considerable interest shown in Darwin's autobiography through the years can be explained by his universally recognized status as one of the most important figures of his time. The autobiography is not considered a literary masterpiece, but it has been read carefully for insights into the character of this seminal mind.

According to Darwin, he wrote his "account of the development of my mind and character with some sketch of my autobiography" to amuse himself and to provide information about himself to his children and grandchildren (21), and, like Trollope and others, he adopts the argument *ex morte*, which apparently allows perfect frankness:

> I have attempted to write the following account of myself, as if I were a dead man in another world looking back at my own life. Nor have I found this difficult, for life is nearly over with me. I have taken no pains about my style of writing. (21)

Compared to the other book-length autobiographies considered in this study, Darwin's is slight, comprising fewer than 150 printed pages. It can be considered an account of life and career, though Darwin does not give a very full account of either. He divides his book into eight unnumbered sections. The first section, following a brief introduction, covers his life from his birth in 1809 up to 1828, the year he entered Cambridge, and the second covers his university years, 1828–31. Although Darwin's narrative in these sections at times seems almost as arbitrarily organized as Ruskin's, with apparently random, isolated memories about family and school life and an extended sketch of his father, "who was in many ways a remarkable man" (28), he establishes at once the line of development that his mind is to take. His "taste for natural history" and "passion for collecting" were well developed by the time he attended day school at the age of eight, and youthful experiments at his home demonstrated an interest in the variability of plants (22–23). These observations establish the story line of personal development as well as the hermeneutic explanation of his life. Darwin's thesis is that his basic qualities of mind are innate rather than learned: "I am inclined to agree with Francis Galton in believing that education and environment produce only a small effect on the mind of anyone, and that most of our qualities are innate" (43).

The story of young Darwin's formal education from the seven years of ill-suited classical studies at a day school near his home, through the two years of haphazard medical study at the University of Edinburgh, to the "wasted" Cambridge years of 1828–32 is a chronicle of aimlessness. Darwin's conscious sense of vocation is described as very hazy and ill defined. Because he thought his inheritance from his father would provide him with a sufficient livelihood, he did not seriously pursue the medical studies at Edinburgh that might have led him to follow the path of his physician father (though he had inclinations in that direction), and he vaguely intended to become a clergyman at Cambridge. Shooting became his principal pursuit in life. However, the retrospective narrator sees a simultaneous "natural" development on an informal level—the boy's continuing passion for collecting during walking and riding tours, both biological and geological, and his personal relationships with prominent scientists at the universities.

The third section, "Voyage of the 'Beagle': From Dec. 27, 1831 to Oct. 2, 1836," records the circumstances that transformed the life of Darwin. None of the turning points in the previously discussed autobiographies was more decisive than this. Through his friendship with Professor Henslow of Cambridge he learned of Captain Fitz-Roy's offer to share his cabin with "any young man who would volunteer to go with him without pay as naturalist to the Voyage of the *Beagle*" (71). Darwin's father opposed his accepting the offer but agreed to relent if "any man of common sense" advised the young man to go. After Darwin had already written a letter declining the offer, his Uncle Josiah Wedgewood successfully intervened on his behalf. "The voyage of the *Beagle* has been by far the most important event in my life and has determined my whole career; yet it depended on so small a circumstance as my uncle offering to drive me 30 miles to Shrewsbury, which few uncles would have done, and on such a trifle as the shape of my nose" (76–77). (Fitz-Roy, "a disciple of Lavater," nearly rejected him because of the unfavorable shape of his nose!)

Ironically, this "most important event" is passed over fairly quickly since Darwin has already described it in detail in his published *Journal*. At this point, the *Autobiography* becomes a commentary on the previous publication, describing its significance and giving personal details that would not have been included in the objective, scientific account: amusing anecdotes, a character sketch of the good-hearted but fiery-tempered Captain Fitz-Roy, and most important, Darwin's interpretation of his personal growth and mental development during the voyage.

The voyage of the *Beagle*, considered as a single event, is not only the turning point in Darwin's self-history but is the first foregrounded event in the narrative. Everything prior to this is background. Because of chance, the innate qualities in the young protagonist could now be developed in definitive ways. During the five years of the voyage, Darwin's powers of observation were increased, as well as his knowledge of both biology and geology (77), and he developed habits of "energetic industry" and "concentration of attention" (78). As his mature habits of mind and love of science gradually increased, his old immature passion for shooting gradually decreased. The author-narrator offers a sweeping explanation: "The primeval instincts of the barbarian slowly yielded to the acquired tastes of the civilized man" (79).

The figure of Darwin as microcosm of mankind does not, however, obscure the essential and concrete results of this rapid evolution of mind and character. Most importantly, Darwin began to publish his observations on natural history, and his *Journal of the Beagle* became his first important publication. Increasingly ambitious to publish and "impress great men" (81), he began his career as the author of scientific publications as soon as he returned to England in October 1836, entering into the most active "two years and three months" of his life, despite recurring spells of the "nervous illness" that was to haunt him for the rest of his life. After arranging for the final publication of his *Journal* and works directly based on it, in July of 1837, "I opened my first note-book for facts in relation to the *Origin of Species*, about which I had long reflected, and never ceased working on for the next twenty years" (83).

After the short section "From My Return to England Oct. 2, 1836 to My Marriage Jan. 29, 1839" (which, despite its title, does not discuss his marriage), Darwin interrupts the chronological sequence of his narrative to discuss his "Religious Belief." In this section, he describes in a general way his gradual movement toward disbelief in Christian doctrine and briefly outlines the theist, agnostic, and vaguely meliorist views that replaced his former beliefs. Here he ties his own development to the historical "spread of skepticism or rationalism during the latter half of my life" (95).

"From My Marriage, January 29, 1839, and My Residence in Upper Gower Street to Our Leaving London and Settling at Down, Sept. 14, 1842" opens with a tribute to his wife, addressed directly to his children, and then continues in "memoir" fashion, referring to scientists, as well as "historians and other literary men" whom he had met in London.

"Residence at Down, from Sept. 14, 1842, to the Present Time, 1876" briefly concludes his personal narrative. He does not regret his increasing seclusion from society at his country retreat but laments his loss of the "power of becoming deeply attached to anyone," even his dear friends Hooker and Huxley. This "grievous loss of feeling" is of course associated with the nervous condition that finally made it impossible to talk with anyone beyond his immediate family without suffering from exhaustion as a result. He finds comfort and enjoyment only in his scientific work, in which he continues to be absorbed. He concludes the section with a statement that is remarkably similar to analogous statements in other Victorian autobiographies: "I have therefore nothing to record during the rest of my life, except the publication of my several books" (115–16). Like so many others, his life story becomes identical with his bibliography.

In the final section, "My Several Publications," Darwin goes back in time to 1844, when he published a book based on the geology of the islands visited by the *Beagle*—followed closely by a revised edition of his *Journal of the Beagle*—to summarize his entire publication history, a narrative in itself. (The original *Journal* had been published in 1839 as part of Fitz-Roy's work.) It is a story of deep absorption and affection for his subjects, some of the most specialized nature, such as the multivolume work on *Cirripedia*, which was the product of an eight-year project. It is also the story of his struggle with illness; for example, he estimates that two of the eight years spent on *Cirripedia* were lost by illness. (Ill health prevented him from attending his father's funeral in 1847.) Darwin's account of writing the *Origin of Species*, although relatively brief, is given with a care for detail reminiscent of Newman's *Apologia*. Working on "true Baconian principles," he had opened his first notebook on the subject in July 1837 (120) and began years of careful research, refusing to write "even the briefest abstract" of his theory until June 1842. Inspired by reading Malthus's *Population* in 1838 to develop his own version of the "struggle for existence" among animals and plants, Darwin had pondered the problem of species modification for several years, and then:

> I can remember the very spot in the road, while in my carriage, when to my joy the solution occurred to me; and this was long after I had come to Down [in September 1842]. The solution, as I believe, is that the modified offspring of all dominant and increasing forms tend to become adapted to many and highly diversified places in the economy of nature. (120–21)

Darwin goes on to carefully outline subsequent developments: the encouragement from Lyell and Hooker to publish; collaboration with Alfred R. Wallace, who had worked out the same theory independently; and publication of the book in November 1859 after years of (felicitous) delay.

Descriptions of subsequent publications of books and articles follow, each with a summary of the research and calculation of the writing time required and in most cases a succinct estimation of its scientific value. Finally, "During this autumn of 1876 I shall publish on the *Effects of Cross- and Self-Fertilization in the Vegetable Kingdom"* and Darwin mentions further plans for reviewing previously published works until his strength is exhausted (133). However, in an addendum made in 1881, he comments on the publication of the previous work and records still further publications, ending with "a little book on *The Formation of Vegetable Mould Through the Action of Worms"* which he has just sent to the publisher (1 May 1881). This final publication is particularly appropriate because it represents the completion of a short paper read before the Geological Society more than forty years before and thus suggests continuity and structural symmetry in Darwin's work as a whole.

But Darwin is not quite through.

> I have now mentioned all the books which I have published, and these have been the milestones in my life, so that little remains to be said. I am not conscious of any change in my mind during the last thirty years, excepting in one point... nor indeed could any change have been expected unless one of general deterioration. (136)

(The one change is his regrettable loss of the ability to appreciate poetry.) He ends with an assessment of his mental powers and method of work.

Darwin's narrative shares many of the characteristics of the autobiographies already discussed. As with Martineau, illness[2] serves to limit and focus his life and work and is central to his formation of a unified self. His illness systematically shuts him off from almost every aspect of life experience except his scientific writing and publication. Not only is he "forced" into seclusion, but he even loses his feelings of affection for old friends, so with the exception of his immediate family, he is isolated from society.

Much as with Trollope, the plot of Darwin's story turns on a single external event, a stroke of good fortune that allows him to develop his innate (fated) abilities and sensibilities in order to become a "civilized" man and the author-scientist known to the public (which in this case is much of the world) through his publications. His habits of life and formula for composition, like Trollope's, become central to the story as his history of self gradually becomes identical to his history of publications. On the other hand, like Newman, he is cautious and circumspect in explaining his development of mind, step by step, relative to his expression of ideas, both privately and publicly, plainly conscious that both the ideas and the development of these ideas are controversial. Like Ruskin, Darwin defines a specific "mode of consciousness" at the root of all his intellectual activities from early youth. For Ruskin, it is to look, feel, and then analyze. For Darwin, it is to collect facts and then group them under general laws (141). In the case of each author, the fundamental formula is seen as generating the narrative of mental activity, but with Darwin, unlike Ruskin, the narrative is a highly developmental one, achieving closure as Darwin becomes the mature scientist.

As already noted, Darwin's narrative of personal development reaches a point of near stasis after the voyage of the *Beagle* and the period of extreme work inspired by that voyage. The section "Religious Belief" that follows his account of the most active period of two years and three months after the voyage serves a double function within the structure of the narrative. First, it quickly describes the course of disbelief, which had "crept over me at a very slow rate" (87). Although the time scheme here is vague, Darwin reports that he had been "quite orthodox" (85) on board the *Beagle* and implies that his subsequent loss of belief occurred during the years in which he was building his theories and his scientific career upon his *Beagle* experiences. Rather than focus on a religious crisis of mind or spirit, however, he refers generally to the gradual process (evolutionary rather than catastrophic) and proceeds to a description of his mature beliefs, not fully formulated until much later in life. Thus the chapter also fulfills a function analogous to the final chapters of Newman and Mill, appropriately so, since the main force of his development in the narrative has been spent. With the controversial religious question out of the way, Darwin can proceed to the short account of his later years, the self-contained publication history, and then the "objective" summary assessment of his strengths and weaknesses as a thinker and writer that becomes his final statement to the reader.

The persona of Darwin's narrator is that of a careful, deliberate man, dedicated to scientific truth. He admits to cherishing the praise of his fellow scientists but claims he "never turned one inch out my course to gain fame" (82). The independently wealthy Darwin is able to pursue his ideals as his vocation.

Though Darwin ostensibly writes to amuse himself and inform

his children, his rhetorical stance is clearly aimed at establishing a correct public version of himself and his works. Most significant is his careful self-portrait of the model scientist in the Baconian tradition, with all appropriate modesty and restraint, and his "objective" assessment of the scientific contribution made by each of his published works. Darwin's awareness of the most controversial aspects of his life and career is also evident. Conscious of the fact that he is perceived by many as a great enemy of traditional Christianity and that even members of his own family, including his wife (87n), are sensitive to his religious position, Darwin devotes a separate section to religion. On the one hand he does not flinch from labeling the Christian belief in Hell for nonbelievers "a damnable doctrine" (87). On the other hand, he emphasizes the great length and difficulty of the process that led to his own position of agnosticism and stresses his own meliorist views—which not only suggest a humanitarianism beyond that of Christian doctrine but also contradict the potential image of a heartless believer in the natural struggle for survival. Furthermore, Darwin as agnostic is in the vanguard of the "remarkable . . . spread of skepticism or rationalism" (95) during his lifetime and thus plays an appropriate part in the cultural evolution of his age.

More specifically, Darwin had to contend with the issue of originality in discussing his all-important *Origin of Species* and the theory of evolution. In his account of the long, painstaking process of composition, already alluded to, he is most careful to document not only the facts surrounding the original publication of his own and Alfred Wallace's independently conceived but "identical" theories but also his attitudes and motives. Darwin even claims, "I cared very little whether men attributed most originality to me or Wallace" (124). On the other hand, he discounts the popular view that the subject of evolution was "in the air" when he published the *Origin*, because he had never come upon a fellow naturalist who "seemed to doubt about the permanence of species" (124). He expresses no remorse for a life devoted to science but regrets not having done more for his fellow men. He says his critics have been fair (though he implies that he may not have received sufficient credit for certain ideas).

Darwin devotes a relatively large amount of space to memories of public men he has known, especially men of science, and his apparently frank evaluations of these men and their contributions has much the same force as Trollope's evaluation of his fellow novelists. Occasionally, there is a touch of nostalgia for the past time of good fellowship parallel to Newman's sketches of old Oxford associates in Darwin's portraits of men in the scientific fraternity—Joseph D. Hooker, Sir Charles Lyell, T. H. Huxley. Other scientists—as well as some literary figures—receive mostly negative assessments. The geologist William Buckland is good-natured but "vulgar and almost coarse" (102), Richard Owen is jealous of Darwin's success (105), Herbert Spencer is "extremely egotistical" and unscientific in his methods (108–9), Carlyle "sneered at almost every one" and held "revolting" views about slavery (113).

Fairly late in his book, for a short space, Darwin suddenly addresses his children directly: "You all know well your mother, and what a good mother she has ever been to all of you" (96). Although these affectionate and intimate paragraphs came at the beginning of the section entitled "From My Marriage...to Our...Settling at Down" and although the entire book is supposed to be addressed to his children, they are so different in sense of audience that the general reader is likely to be startled when he comes upon them. Darwin soon slips back into his characteristic, more distanced voice, and does not directly address his children again.

The distance between Darwin the author-narrator and his protagonist, even in descriptions of early childhood, is not especially great, in spite of the fact that the pre-*Beagle* Darwin is rather shiftless and that his potential for making a significant contribution to science is latent, presaged only by his "innate" habits of observation and collecting natural objects, as well as the apparently instinctive interest in him taken by certain mentors. With Darwin there is no myth of the miserable, deprived child. Although he loses his mother early in life, the youthful protagonist is guided by his wise and generous father (who does not seem to be resented for nearly preventing Darwin's *Beagle* adventure). Grammar school, spent within walking distance of home, is not especially educational but not traumatic, either. The Cambridge years are educationally barren but carefree and happy, largely spent in the highly pleasurable pastime of shooting. The narrator is curious about the innate qualities of his young protagonist, qualities that in their natural unfolding prepare him for the fortuitous opportunity to become an important scientist. In most characteristics, the protagonist is average or even below average, but he is a persistent observer and collector of nature facts. Near the end of the book, the narrator evaluates the strengths and weaknesses of his mature protagonist, who is now identical with himself. He is a poor critic with a bad memory, but in addition to his powers of observation he is industrious and ambitious to gain the esteem of his fellow naturalists, has a strong desire to group facts under natural laws. The last sentence of the book leaves the impression of a man to whom fortune has been kind: "With such moderate abilities as I possess, it is truly surprising that thus I should have influenced to a considerable extent the beliefs of scientific men on some important points" (145). Yet the protagonist Darwin is not presented without a touch of typically Victorian regret. Even the chronic illness that has "annihilated several years" of his life has had the salutary effect of saving him from "the distractions of society and amusement" (144), but there is no corresponding compensation for the "curious and lamentable loss of the higher aesthetic tastes" (139) that has overtaken him in his later years. He associates his loss of pleasure in poetry and music—and thus some loss of happiness—with the capacity of his mind to act as a "machine for grinding general laws out of large collections of facts" (139) but speculates that a regular program of reading poetry and listening to music might have helped to keep alive that part of his brain "on which the higher tastes depend" (139), a program similar to Mill's deliberate cultivation of the emotions.

Darwin's *Autobiography* is a slender volume not only because of his relatively succinct style, perhaps appropriate to a scientist in Darwin's tradition and far removed from the garrulousness of some autobiographers, but also because past time is severely condensed within the present time of the book. Of course, Darwin admits to a "hazy" memory and wonders what he must have thought about on the long walks he took as a youth (25), but he does not place a great emphasis on the loss of memory and access to past time. In fact, past time prior to his *Beagle* voyage can be easily summarized, because there are few essential incidents to describe. The all-important voyage of the *Beagle* has already been recorded in a published *Journal*, so Darwin need not dwell on that. After his return to England, Darwin soon becomes the author whose life is adequately described by his publication record. Not only does the story of self-development come to an end, but even memories based on social interaction becomes largely irrelevant to his secluded life. Thus Darwin manages to write an exceedingly narrow res gestae account. Nevertheless, much like Gibbon, Darwin does recall with exceptional clarity a few key epiphany-like moments related to the development of his ideas and works and associated with concrete visual images. One of the most remarkable instances of visual memory recorded in the book is the "exact appearance" of certain posts, old trees, and banks at Cambridge where he captured beetles (63). And, as already seen, he "can remember the very spot in the road, whilst in my carriage" where the solution to the problem of the modification of species first occurred to him (120–21).

Structurally, Darwin's *Autobiography* implicitly makes a claim for universality in much the way that Newman's does, though his identity as a scientist makes comparison with the positivists Mill and Martineau more obvious. On a social level, Darwin is functioning within the history of nineteenth-century British institutions. His life and work have a meaning in the context of contemporary scientific thought. On a higher level, Darwin is participating in the progressive movement toward a better world for man through science. As his description of self-development during the voyage of the *Beagle* implies, Darwin's individual life story stands in relation to the history of civilization as the development of the human embryo does to the entire evolutionary process.

Chapter 8

Sir Walter Besant, *Autobiography* (1902)

It is tempting to read Walter Besant's life-and-career autobiography as a slighter and paler version of the Victorian novelist's autobiography as established by Trollope. Like Trollope, Besant spent much of his time in his fictional "dreamworld," identified strongly with his imaginary characters, insisted on treating the writer as a professional and practical businessman, and offered plentiful practical advice to aspiring writers. Like Trollope, he virtually excluded his inner life, though he did not make such a rhetorical point of it. To read the self-history of Besant exclusively against that of the better-known Trollope, however, would be to ignore its many individual qualities.

Besant (1836–1901) is not widely read or studied today, but he was a prolific writer who published several successful novels, beginning in the 1870s. One unusual aspect of his career is his collaboration with coauthor James Rice in nearly all his fiction until Rice's fatal illness in 1881. Besant was also known for his involvement in various social issues, including the legal rights of authors, and for his ambitious projected survey of London, which remained unfinished at his death.

His *Autobiography*, written in the last year of his life, also was never quite finished. Besant died before he could revise the drafts of his final chapters. The book was published with a long preface by S. Squire Sprigge that attempted to soften the effect of some of Besant's outspoken opinions—severe criticism of literary critics and certain publishing practices and, especially, his invective against organized religion—by suggesting that the author would have qualified or softened them in his final draft.

Besant's autobiography is marked by two prominent formal characteristics that call attention to themselves. One is a tension between narrative and thematic structure even greater than that found in the previous works we have examined. As we have seen, both Martineau and Trollope insert thematic essays into their autobiographies; furthermore, most of the autobiographers include memoirs and reminiscences of one kind or another that interrupt the narrative of self-development, and they commonly end their books with some sort of Augustinian coda. Besant goes even further, however, and makes his final five chapters primarily thematic, as we will see.

The second characteristic is more unusual. Besant's first two chapters, both entitled "Child and Boy," have a mythic and dreamlike quality and are dominated by a heavily nostalgic sense of place. This in itself is not strange, and Besant's portrait of his home city of Portsmouth[1] and its suburbs (he was born in Portsea) may remind one of similarly nostalgic descriptions in Ruskin and elsewhere. Also, he prefaces his account by listing the reasons why the circumstances of his childhood were advantageous for one who is to be a writer—a child with an inventive turn of mind is born into a large middle-class family in a busy town. However, in his description of the Portsmouth environment, Besant introduces several long quotations from his novels, especially *By Celia's Arbor* (1878), which apparently serve as substitutes for recollections by the retrospective author-narrator. Of course, he says that the novel's passages are based on personal experience, and even remarks that "in recalling those days it is difficult to separate them from the imaginary characters of my novel. . . . It is not myself who is running across that heath, but those two boys, who share between them my identity" (44). But the first-person narrator of the novel is somewhat exotic, the son of Polish exiles, and though Besant apparently incorporated many realistic details of Portsmouth geography and culture into the book and even introduced supporting characters who were modeled after real people, his descriptions are somewhat distanced not only from his inner life as a boy but from family life or interpersonal relationships. Also, the notion that the two fictional boys "share between them" his identity seems vaguely schizophrenic. But even this curious device is representative of the autobiographer's practice of privileging books over life: Besant writes that "[i]n recalling those days it is difficult to separate them from the imaginary characters of my novel." Here he may be adopting the voice of an aged, absentminded man, but he is also expressing the sort of affection for his publications that we have seen in the other autobiographies and is reclaiming or symbolically reinternalizing that part of himself which he had made public.

Besant does give brief, very favorable descriptions of his mother and father, but he gives few details of family life in relating a few childhood anecdotes. He notes his failure to learn his catechism from his teacher, his vague childhood ambition to be a clergyman. Though Besant introduces other quotations from his novels later in the book, they do not appear so obtrusive as those in the first two chapters.

Chapter 3 describes Besant's life as "School-Boy" at Stockwell Grammar School (located in a suburb of London), which he entered in 1851 at the age of fifteen. This chapter is the first of three concisely organized chapters on his formal education. Here begins Besant's fascination with the city of London, which is to remain with him for the rest of his life. He criticizes the ineffectual teaching methods of his school and lists his old school fellows.

Chapter 4 is devoted to Besant's life at King's College, London, which he entered in 1854, and chapter 5 to his experiences at Christ's Church, Cambridge. Although his purpose was to "enter holy orders," at King's College he developed ambitions as a writer and fantasized about becoming a great poet such as Tennyson. The chapter on student life at Cambridge is particularly rich in anecdotes about the antiquated regimen there and in references to teachers and fellow students. The effect of Cambridge on him was "wholly and unreservedly beneficial" (98), widening his mind "in every imaginable way" (97). In terms of his ambitions and professional goals, it made a career in the church impossible (as he realized in retrospect) and convinced him that he would have to read more before he could hope to be a writer.

Chapter 6, "A Tramp Abroad," takes Besant, after graduation, very quickly through his failed attempt to become a journalist in London and his subsequent acceptance of a school mastership at Leamington. However, most of this chapter consists of nostalgic anecdotes concerning a walking tour of Europe that Besant took with friends during his tenure at Leamington. Besant's mastership was soon in trouble because its continuation was dependent on his imminent ordination. As the day of ordination approached, Besant prepared himself "for perjury, because by this time I understood that the white tie would choke me" (109). But he was rescued from his miserable position by a fortunate opportunity parallel to those offered Trollope and Darwin: "And then—oh! happiness!—a door of release was thrown open" (109). Through a friend, he was offered his choice of two colonial professorships—he accepted the one in Mauritius. "Though I could not suspect the fact, I was about to equip myself . . . for the real solid work of my life, which has been the observation of men and women, and the telling of stories about them" (110).

Chapter 7, "L'Ile de France," describes Besant's six-year stay as a mathematics professor in Mauritius. The chapter, beginning with the adventurous outbound journey on the big liner *Indus*, is much like a travelogue. Besant writes very little about his professional duties but tells a series of anecdotes about the "strange, colorful, picturesque kind of life that one led there" (121), concentrating especially on the interesting characters he met among the masters, the missionaries, and the island planters. Besant, the developing novelist, was "writing all the time" (140). He wrote essays, most of which he tore up, verse that he never published, and a first, abortive novel. He also studied Old French and established himself as a scholar in French literature. Mauritius was hardly like Trollope's Ireland—the tropical climate was unhealthy and susceptible to hurricanes and waterspouts, a plague of tropical fever killed thousands of islanders while he was there, and Besant himself was given to spells of "melancholia" toward the end of his stay. Nevertheless, the six-year stay in Mauritius functions in Besant's narrative plot as a liberating turning point in his life and "lively" anecdotes of island life illustrate his developing powers as an observer and a writer.

In Chapter 8, "England Again: The Palestine Exploration Fund," Besant "began life again" in England at the age of thirty-one, but he admonishes himself, "Let me be always thankful for my colonial experiences" (149). The six and one-half years in Mauritius "had completely changed the whole current of my thoughts—my views of society, order, religion, everything" (148). Two significant events occurred in 1868. Besant published a book on early French poetry that established him as a published author in a specialized literary field, and, even more importantly, he accepted a post as secretary to the Society for the Systematic and Scientific Exploration of Palestine, a position that was to last for eighteen years. Much like Mill's position in the East India Company and Trollope's in the post office, the post "enabled me to realize my dream of a literary life without dependence, and therefore degradation" (166). Much of this chapter is devoted to colorful anecdotes of his experiences in the Society through the years, and the chronological flow of the narrative is broken at the point of Besant's reintegration into England in favor of a thematic format that becomes dominant in the remainder of the book.

Chapter 9, "First Steps in the Literary Career—and Later" goes back to 1868 to show how Besant got his feet on "the lower rungs of the ladder" in his literary career and how he "began to climb." On the basis of his first book on French literature, Besant gained a reputation that allowed him to write for magazines, reviews, and newspapers, and then he published a second book, *The French Humourists*, in 1873. Besant goes on to describe his later critical and biographical work and mentions some of the literary acquaintances he met during the 1870s.

In chapter 10, "The Start in Fiction: Critics and Criticasters," Besant again retraces his steps to the beginning of his "second life" in London in order to narrate his career specifically as a writer of fiction. His story, "Titania's Farewell," written for the Christmas number of *Once a Week* in 1869, gained for him a reputation as a writer of fiction. "To me, this flimsy trifle became of the utmost importance, because it changed the whole current of my life" (181). In short, Besant escaped the "barren and dreary" course of the critic to become a creative writer. Soon he was collaborating with Rice on a novel, *Ready Money Mortiboy*, which was a popular success when it was published in 1872.[2] By 1881, when Rice was forced to retire due to illness, the two men were coauthors of nine published novels, as well as a collection of short stories.

Rice's death from throat cancer in 1882 is both tragic and liberating for Besant. It is at this point in his narrative, beginning with chapter 11, "The Novelist with a Free Hand," that Besant's life, like those of many other Victorian autobiographers, merges with his bibliography: "My life between 1882 and 1900 is a simple chronicle of work done" (198). This chronicle of "eighteen novels in eighteen years" is most Trollopian, complete with descriptions of composition techniques and the publication process, and evaluations of his own works. *Dorothy Foster* is "by far the best" of his novels (204). The summing up of accomplishments at the end of this chapter effectively ends the narrative line. "My course as a novelist—or anything else—is now nearly finished" (212).

Chapter 12, "The Society of Authors and Other Societies," which narrates the separate story of the professional society that Besant helped to organize and to which he devoted much attention and energy in his later years, was never properly revised for inclusion in the autobiography, though it is clear that Besant meant to include it (215n). This thematic chapter also includes Besant's description and defence of other favorite societies, the Masons and the short-lived Rabelais Club.

Besant's account of his philanthropic work in chapter 13, especially his part in founding the People's Palace in the East End of London,[3] is directly related to his career as a novelist. In researching his sociological novels *All Sorts and Conditions of Men* and *Children of Gibeon*, he became involved in issues concerning the London poor.

Chapter 14 outlines Besant's work in progress, "The Survey of London," which he hoped would be published during his lifetime, and chapter 15 describes the operations of the Atlantic Union, which he had helped to found in 1900 and which was intended to foster better relations and understanding among Englishmen, Irishmen, Scotsmen, Australians, Canadians, citizens of any British colony, and Americans. These two chapters, then, even though thematic in structure, represent Besant's current interests at the time of writing and, brief and sketchy as they are, help to complete the self-portrait of an industrious man still hard at work toward the end of his life.

The last chapter is something else again. "Conclusion: The Conduct of Life and the Influence of Religion" functions as Besant's Augustinian coda, a final "few words befitting the close of a life" (273). His reference to F. D. Maurice, the principal thinker who enabled him to "shovel away the evangelical rubbish" (279), recalls his earlier chapters on his Cambridge days and the slow, almost unconscious process that finally made the prospect of ordination unbearable to him. At Leamington, it had been rumored that Besant was not sound on the Thirty-nine Articles, especially the doctrine of the Atonement, which he most vociferously attacks in this final chapter. In fact, as early as his story of boyhood in the early chapters, the anti-Evangelical theme has been present in his admiring portrait of his father, who resisted the Calvinistic "nonsense" surrounding him. In the Mauritius chapter, Besant has related the experiences of disillusioned Christian missionaries he met and wondered how many other similar cases may exist (131). Thus Besant's autobiography contains suggestive segments of a thematic autobiography such as Gosse's *Father and Son* within the generalized life-and-career framework. Once again, as with Martineau, the last chapter of one's autobiography is seen as the peculiarly appropriate forum for the ultimate message to one's audience. But there has been little emphasis on Besant's growth of mind or formulation of a worldview throughout the narrative. He merely takes the opportunity to strike one more blow at an old enemy, Calvinistic religiosity,[4] and offers his own rather mild, tolerant, vaguely deistic religious views.

The events that serve as plot functions in Besant's life-and-career narrative are primarily external. The turning point of his life, his six years' colonial experience, is much like Trollope's assignment to Ireland and Darwin's voyage aboard the *Beagle* and like them is a result of chance that allows his innate potential to develop in congenial ways. Mental development is part of the story but not foregrounded.

Besant does not, like Trollope, emphasize his anticonfessional stance. In fact, Besant's narrative is largely free of the kind of metadiscourse that the genre seems to encourage. Besant as author-narrator assumes that his autobiography is not required to reveal intimate details of his inner life or his private domestic life. Like Trollope, he alludes to a private dreamworld where he spends much of his time with his fictional creations (202) and refers to those details of private life that relate to his career, but there is no further description of interior experience, and he refers to his marriage, wife, and children in passing, and only in relation to his career as novelist. Only in his last paragraph does he directly confront the confessional issue: "Looking back, as I have done in these chapters, I remember a good many mistakes—some things even which I should be ashamed to set down in this page. The book is not one of confessions" (284).

And yet Besant's final philosophical-theological chapter implies a sagelike level to his autobiography that is absent from Trollope's: "And so I leave my belief and my life" (284). The "simple" doctrine that he expounds in his final chapter is much less emphatic than his trenchant criticism of conventional Christianity, both the "pitiless and horrible" Calvinistic doctrine that was popular in his youth and the absurd ecclesiastical hierarchy and mystique of the priesthood that is associated with the Catholic as well as the English church.

The distance between Besant the narrator and his protagonist is exceedingly great in the early chapters, when actual boyhood experiences are confused with—or displaced by—fictional ones. Anecdotes of personal life grow increasingly sharp and clear as Besant passes through his school years, his tour of the Continent, and his colonial experiences, though even concerning Mauritius, much exotic material has been lost to his memory. Once the protagonist is back in England, anecdotes of personal experiences give way to generalized summaries of career development, memoirs of people met, and thematic essays. Besant's development as a novelist is not so dramatic as Trollope's, not only because Trollope's reputation as a writer was higher and because Trollope did all he could to dramatize his story of success, but at least partially because it consists of several intermediate and somewhat overlapping stages—early unsuccessful attempts at poetry and fiction, critical and historical work, first publication of fiction, coauthorship of fiction, independent career as a novelist. Since Besant is not tracing the development of a central idea or intellectual position, the author-narrator does not scrutinize his protagonist too carefully during the succeeding stages of growth or take pains to document the course of his mental development. For the most part, Besant does not strongly define the character of his past selves. An exception to this generalization may be found in the personal anecdotes associated with adventurous manhood—the walking tour of Europe and the subsequent career in Mauritius. Nowhere does he go far in analyzing the motives of his protagonist, however. The author-narrator, then, dominates his young, undeveloped protagonist, allowing him little of a separate existence within the book. Only a few details such as his shortsightedness (and thus his failure to properly appreciate nature or compete successfully in ball games) are vividly conveyed. Of course, Besant's blurring of childhood experience is only an extreme case of the usual tendency, but the opposite of Ruskin's technique whereby the child protagonist seems to overshadow the narrator.

Besant's rhetorical stance in his autobiography is similar to that of Trollope, although his particular opinions are often quite different. That is, the author's life and work themselves exemplify the advice he gives the reader, particularly that addressed to the specialized audience of young aspiring writers. Although he is modest about his own literary accomplishments, he maintains that he is in the tradition of the masters—Fielding, Smollett, Scott, Thackeray, Dickens, (Charles) Reade (212)—who began with *stories* and not character analyses. Trollope, who was apt to stress character rather than story, is one of the notable exclusions from the list. Like Trollope, however, Besant is proud of his industrious work habits and takes a practical, businesslike approach to writing. The aspirant should first obtain a salaried position that will provide him with the necessary leisure to write. "Never at any time was I dependent on my pen for a subsistence" (166). He, too, shares with the reader his own procedure for writing a novel, somewhat less regimented than Trollope's (199–200).

His insistence on the professional status of the writer is reinforced by his separate treatment of the Society of Authors. Besant's "crusade" for the legal rights of authors as well as his work in other philanthropic and social areas, and even the historical-sociological interest behind his Survey of London project—all these forms of public engagement, foregrounded in the later thematic chapters of his autobiography, are seen as important aspects of Besant's selfhood and together define his relationship with the English public. This aspect of the autobiography detracts from the unity of the novelist's story but is in fact consistent with Besant's general reputation as writer and reformer. Unlike Mill, Martineau, Spencer, and other generalists, he does not have a controlling philosophic point of view to give coherence to his various projects, but he does convey a strong sense of social commitment that implies an overarching meliorist narrative of history. And his story of compulsive writing and publishing is grounded in the same ideology of work and duty that is conveyed by many of the other Victorian autobiographers.

Besant's rhetoric occasionally moves beyond the blunt, no-nonsense prose of Trollope into invective. Though he does not use the autobiography to praise or blame particular individuals to the extent that many autobiographers do, his jeremiads against "ignorant reviewers" and "criticasters" as a class and against evangelical Christianity are reminiscent of late Carlylean rhetorical excesses. Besant's combative stance is underscored when he lists along with instances of his overall happy life—domestic peace, literary success, favor, friends—a "whole army of enemies," including the "spiritualist fraud," the "sticky sentimentalist," and the "shrieking sisterhood" (214). (Besant had satirized the feminists of his day in his novel *The Revolt of Man*).

Overall, it can be said that Besant's *Autobiography* exhibits relatively little of the tension between the retrospective author-narrator and the protagonist, between present time and past time, between selfhood and environment, between the uniqueness of life experience and universal meanings, that is characteristic of many Victorian autobiographies. Put another way, Besant as author-narrator does not struggle hard to reconcile these oppositions. However, the autobiography, immersed as it is in social history, does imply a meliorist vision of life. Besant presents himself as one of society's tireless workers in the cause of clearing away the rubbish of sham and superstition.

Chapter 9

Herbert Spencer, *An Autobiography* (1904)

Herbert Spencer's is one of the longest Victorian autobiographies, consisting of two large volumes. Spencer intended that the first volume should complete the history of his "engineering and miscellaneous life" and the second should begin with his literary life, but that plan had to be modified by his publishers, since his account of his career as a writer, which began in his late forties, is much longer than his account of the earlier period. He wrote the book during his midfifties to late sixties, the bulk of it toward the end of this time.[1] The initial draft was dictated to a secretary, his usual method of composition during the latter stages of his career, at least partially due to his ill health. Spencer had been subject to a severe nervous disorder (however hypochondriacal it may have been) since early childhood, a condition that in his later years seriously restricted not only his writing but all mental activity, including reading for pleasure and even conversation. In his opening note Spencer makes it clear that, although a few advance copies were shown to friends, the *Autobiography* is intended for posthumous publication, citing the "frankness" of the book (ix–x). Spencer died in 1903, and his *Autobiography* was published in the following year. By this time, his reputation as one of the dominant intellectual figures of the late nineteenth century had begun to fall precipitously.[2]

Although it gives a useful account of his career and publications, provides an interesting glimpse of early railroading in England, and refers to major figures such as T. H. Huxley, Mary Ann Evans (George Eliot),[3] and George H. Lewes, Spencer's *Autobiography* has never been considered a literary masterpiece. Much of the narrative could be described as plodding, a quality that is probably related to his method of dictation with insufficient revision. He habitually strings together quotations from innumerable letters instead of summarizing their contents. Mundane events, such as house visits, are described in some detail, as though Spencer were afraid of failing to be thorough. Spencer also notes at several points (sometimes with regret, sometimes with pride), that he never had a single English language lesson in his life. At any rate, he clutters his verbose writing style with awkward passive constructions and consistently substitutes nominalizations for active verbs. His clumsy style is ironic in light of his interest in the issue of writing style and his self-identification as a writer. In at least one sense, however, Spencer's is among the most intriguing Victorian autobiographies, for in it he merges life experience with theory, so that his life becomes an argument for his work in the most thoroughgoing way.

Like Martineau's, Spencer's *Autobiography* is also a full-scale treatment of life and literary career in the Gibbon tradition. His given motive for writing it is typical: "No one whose name has been much before the public can escape having his life written: if he does not do it himself someone else will do it for him." He alone can supply the narrative "with anything like completeness" and furnish the "verifying and illustrative materials" to go with it (2:334). In his preface, Spencer terms his work a "natural history," and in some sections of the book, it seems as though the narrator is merely acting as an objective researcher, piecing together bits of physical evidence—in this case, documents, principally letters. Extensive quotations from various letters are strung together in an almost skeletal narrative. Spencer describes his method of composition: he dictates the notes that will be revised into his narrative and inserts these pages between the letters and other documents from which he will quote (2:335). This method is at least partially explained by the nervous illness that has plagued him since his thirties, and during the time of composition has so nearly incapacitated him that he can work only for very short periods of time—in some cases, only a few minutes at a time and less than an hour a day. However, this characteristic of the text also reflects the narrator's "objective" scientific values, common Victorian views concerning documentation, and his mistrust of memory.

Spencer's narrative scheme is doggedly chronological. He struggles against discursive drift away from a chronological sequence of life events in a persistent effort to control his material. Although he calls attention to overlaps in his narrative (2:283), they are relatively few. He is nothing if not methodical. The first volume contains a long sort of preamble, giving the completest possible genealogical account of his forebears in a manner reminiscent of Gibbon, divided into three chapters: "Extraction," "Grandparents," and "Parents."

After alluding to the vanity of genealogies (1:3), Spencer gives an account of his ancestors primarily focused on the "nonconformist tendency" or rather conformity to higher principles (whether to Deity or "Natural principles") and other related traits that he finds in both his maternal and paternal line of ancestry (1:12). He anticipates the narrative of his own life by outlining his dominant character traits of disregard for authority, the placement of "superhuman" principles above human ones, and the contemplation of remote rather than immediate results, all of which he had apparently inherited from his forebears.

A five-chapter part 1 then covers seventeen years of childhood and youth, from 1820 to 1837. In some ways, Spencer's narrative of his formative years is similar to Mill's. As in the case of Mill, he was greatly influenced by his father, an eccentric schoolmaster hampered by delicate health. The major difference is that Spencer was not required to adhere to a strict educational discipline and developed a fiercely independent spirit early on. His father did reinforce his tendency to "regard everything as naturally caused" and to think for himself (1:101). Spencer's ingrained rebelliousness is illustrated when at the age of thirteen he runs away from his Uncle Thomas's school and returns home. Unlike Mill, who relied on his memory to reproduce reading lists and precise intellectual influences, Spencer has only vague memories of childhood (including his childhood education) and concentrates on the formation of general traits such as the ability to become absorbed in a single problem and the habit of "castlebuilding" (1:85–86). Already in describing his early development, Spencer relies on documents—primarily, letters to his father, written from school—to an extraordinary extent in recalling not only events but attitudes and emotions from the past. When he comes to a gap in those records, the narrative becomes tentative and vague, as during the period 1836–37.

At the end of part 1, young Spencer's projected career as a teacher (urged by his father) is interrupted by his Uncle William's offer to find a place for him with a railroad company in London. This is the first turning point of Spencer's career. The four chapters of part 2 cover the years 1837–41 and Spencer's life to the age of twenty-one. Working as an assistant engineer, he moved from one position to another. His post as an engineering secretary for several months in 1840 became another turning point (1:175), giving him considerable writing experience. But after a further nomadic period of engineering work, he became "alienated" from his employer (1:210–11) and returned home to Derby.

Although Spencer claims he had no plans of writing books during this time (1:199), his incessant analysis of his own attitudes, abilities, and behavior foregrounds patterns that are to recur throughout his life. His preoccupation with the physical causes of things and habit of daydreaming or "castlebuilding" encourage a stream of ideas for mechanical inventions and mathematical and geometrical speculations. His relative isolation from others is underscored by a brusque social manner. Interestingly, Spencer comes closer than he ever does again to developing a romantic relationship during this period (1:194).

Part 3 covers the period 1841–44, beginning with Spencer's move home. A major motive for returning was to help his father develop his plans for an electromagnetic engine. Although this project proved to be unsound, Spencer interprets his "seemingly foolish" decision as a step that even in retrospect saved him from "a humdrum, and not very prosperous, life as a civil engineer" (1:217). The most significant event in this block of time is the series of letters entitled "The Proper Sphere of Government" that Spencer began to write to the *Nonconformist* during a stay with his uncle and former teacher at Hinton in 1842. These letters were later to become the basis of *Social Statics*, Spencer's first major work and the key to his later *Principles of Psychology*. They constituted "the first step to another kind of life" (1:242–43).

From this point on (less than midway through the first volume), there is no doubt about the dominant narrative line of Spencer's autobiography. Although he did a bit more engineering work and dabbled in various projects of intellect and invention, young Spencer was now moving inexorably toward a literary career. He even fantasized about founding a new journal to be entitled *The Philosopher*. More than earlier, Spencer the narrator mentions certain books he remembers reading during this period—Mill's *System of Logic*, Carlyle's *Sartor Resartus*—but, as before, even when his reaction to the book was favorable, he admits little or no intellectual influence.

"Anything like passive receptivity is foreign to my nature; and there results an unusually small tendency to be affected by others' thoughts" (1:277).

Part 4 covers the years 1844–48 and takes Spencer up to the age of twenty-eight. His brief "sub-editorship" for James Wilson and *The Pilot* in 1844 gave him a taste of journalism. (During this time he partially read and quickly rejected Kant's arguments in *The Critique of Pure Reason*.) Then Spencer had a last fling at engineering: first, a time of fieldwork, followed by his involvement in the railroad schemes of engineer William Prichard, which involved giving testimony before parliamentary committees during this time of rapid proliferation of railways and complicated investment schemes. In 1846, he gave up engineering for good (1:345) and began to prepare for his first book, *Social Statics*, though he still did not plan to make writing his profession (1:350) and spent much of his time with various calculations, schemes, and inventions. In 1848, at the age of twenty-eight, he felt "stranded" (1:370). Finally, Spencer was once again employed in an editorial position, this time by *The Economist*, and he made another beginning in journalism. In retrospect, this time of "miscellaneous activities" is one of "spontaneous development."

Part 5 (1848–53) begins with an account of the journalistic duties that were to lead him, "step by step, to [his] special business in life" (1:387). In his new position Spencer began to meet important intellectuals of the day, people such as James Anthony Froude, Francis W. Newman, and, most significantly because of his subsequent long friendship, George H. Lewes. His editorial duties were light enough to permit him to continue his own writing projects, and he had nearly finished *Social Statics* by the spring of 1850. Spencer leaves no doubt as to the central role in his life that writing and publication were to play. "The offspring of the mind, like the offspring of the body, are apt to become objects of engrossing interest to which all other objects are subordinated" (1:406). Like his fellow philosopher Mill, and unlike the novelist Trollope, Spencer's primary motive for writing is never to make money but rather to communicate his ideas. At this point in the narrative the protagonist begins a long struggle to publish his books in an atmosphere of financial strain and uncertainty that will last for most of his career. The narrator Spencer's treatment of the publication process will be repeated throughout the remainder of the autobiography: a description of the often difficult arrangements for publication, a summary of the main ideas of his work (often, as in this case, with a specific disavowal of influences, especially that of Auguste Comte), and a reference to the book's critical reception (often, as in this case, with a lengthy "model" review that *should* have been published by the critics but was not). In spite of the lack of worthy criticism, however, Spencer was pleased with the overall favorable reception of *Social Statics*.

Following the publication of his book, Spencer was largely "inactive" for about a year and contemplated emigration to New Zealand (1:428–30). However, partially through the influence of Lewes and Mary Ann Evans, with whom he now became acquainted, he began to develop a greater interest in philosophy. But most important during this time was his discovery of von Baer's formula for the "course of development through which every plant and animal passes—the change from homogeneity to heterogeneity" (1:445). Spencer embraced this idea, which was to be crucial to much of his later work.

In 1852, Spencer, at the age of thirty-one, began to publish actively in journals. "The Development Hypothesis" and "A Theory of Population Deduced from the General Law of Animal Fertility" both indicated the future direction of his thought. He also wrote his essay "Style" and several others. He continued to develop his well-known relationship with Evans, though he says he rejected her enthusiasm for Comte's ideas, and began a long-lasting friendship with T. H. Huxley.

In 1853, Spencer left *The Economist* and entered a transitional stage of life during which the later stages of his career were determined. Influenced by the example of his Uncle Thomas, whose death was brought on by overwork, Spencer chose "life" over "work" (1:477). A small inheritance from his uncle helped him make the decision to give up his subordinate position at *The Economist* and take a long holiday.

The sixth and final part of volume 1 covers Spencer's life from age thirty-three through thirty-seven. This time is transitional not only in the formation of ideas that would carry him into his later career (1:496); in a tragic sense, the "cardiac disturbances" that followed his tour of Switzerland in 1853 began a pattern of periodic illnesses that were to hound him for the rest of his life (1:502).

Before describing a new series of journal articles, Spencer pauses to make a theoretical statement about his autobiographical narrative:

> I have sought to give more prominence than usual to the delineation of ideas and the manifestations of sentiments; and I have aimed to show, directly or by implication, the relations of these to innate traits, to education, and to circumstances. In the life of the man of action an account of external events naturally occupies the first place; but in the life of the man of thought, the first place should, I think, be occupied by an account of internal events. (1:506)

In this way, Spencer justifies the inclusion of relatively long summaries and extracts of his articles and books—to show the development of his thought, specifically, the development hypothesis, his particular concept of evolution, whereby there is a universal movement from the simple to the complex, the criterion of complexity being differentiation of the parts and their integration, a sort of cosmic antientropic movement, in animate as well as inanimate nature. Spencer had arrived at this "doctrine" by January of 1855 (1:538) and during the remainder of his career applied it to one branch of knowledge after another.

He published his second book, *The Principles of Psychology*, in 1855. About the same time, he suffered another serious illness, and "health, in the full sense of the word, was never again to be overtaken" (1:545). Once again, Spencer writes the reasonable review of his book that should have been written by the critics (1:546).

After partially recovering from his illness, Spencer took his doctor's advice to end his practice of living alone and moved in with a family (1:582). He began once more to publish journal articles. His 1857 essay "Progress" for the *Westminster Review* is particularly important since it became the first installment of his massive *Synthetic Philosophy*, which was to occupy much of his career.

Part 7, the first of the second volume, covers the years 1856–60, during which Spencer worked steadily on his *Philosophy*. Even in the early parts of his self-narrative, Spencer implies that his protagonist is fated to become a writer and thinker, principally by emphasizing the dominant personality traits that would lead him to consistently look for natural causation of things and to think for himself. From this point on, however, the narrator becomes almost obsessed with his protagonist's development. After a lengthy summary of his life and thought up to his late thirties, he pauses to reflect:

On glancing over these stages it is, indeed, observable that the advance towards a complete conception of evolution was itself a process of evolution. At first, there was simply an unshaped belief in the development of living things.... The extension of von Baer's formula expressing the development of each organism ... as parts of a whole, exemplified the process of integration. With advancing integration there went ... advancing heterogeneity.... And then the indefinite idea of progress passed into the definite idea of evolution, ... a physically-determined transformation conforming to ultimate laws of force. Not until setting down as above the successive stages of thought was I myself aware how naturally each stage had prepared the way for the next.... It now seems that there was an almost inevitable transition to that coherent body of beliefs which soon took place. (2:14)[4]

After further reflection and analysis, Spencer goes on to outline the comprehensive "System of Philosophy," which he was already planning at this point in his career, and of which most subsequent individual publications would be a part. One can scarcely imagine a more appropriate device for the marriage of hermeneutics and narrative of life and career. Spencer writes, "It is clear that the first days of 1858 saw the inception of the undertaking to which the rest of my life was to be devoted" (2:21).

Unfortunately for Spencer, the inheritance from his uncle had been depleted by this time, and he was unsuccessful in his attempt to obtain a sinecure through political contacts. He decided upon a plan of subscription to support his massive writing project and, particularly encouraged by the support he had found in America, was fairly successful in attracting subscribers (2:61). He began his volume entitled *First Principles* at age forty (2:67).

Part 8, covering the years 1860–67, shows a man of increasingly ill health narrowing the routine and the interests of his life in order to conserve his physical and intellectual energies for his work, though he continued his social contact with close friends. By now, Spencer was composing exclusively by dictating to an amanuensis for limited periods of time under strictly controlled circumstances. Spencer's scheme of subscription was not proving to be a financial success, but fortunately he received another inheritance—from a second uncle (William)—which enabled him to continue writing. *First Principles* was published in 1862, and Spencer was disappointed by the lack of attention it received (2:85–86).

He then turned to the subject of biology. By the time his second volume of *Biology* was published in 1867, Spencer was so disturbed by misconceived reviews of his works that he directed his publisher not to issue review copies. His financial predicament had worsened, also, but a decision to cease publishing his works was averted by a program of financial aid from his American supporters (2:166). The deaths of his father and then his mother increased his sense of isolation and loneliness.

Part 9 (1867–74) covers Spencer's revision of *First Principles* and his composition of *Psychology* and *Descriptive Sociology*. Early in this section, he summarizes the development of his thought during the period 1850–65. This year-by-year account is somewhat redundant, however, repeating much of the information given in the summary near the beginning of the second volume. Much of this section is taken up with accounts of social visits, bouts with illness, and his 1868 tour of Italy.

Part 10 (1874–79) begins with yet another "retrospective glance" (2:321–22), this time, however, with the specific purpose of introducing Spencer's account of writing *Descriptive Sociology*, an "extra" book that was not part of the *Synthetic Philosophy* series. He recalls his early and continuing "politico-ethical" interest in issues though he had spent many years writing on the "simpler" and more basic sciences (2:322). The process of composition began with Spencer's sorting and classifying a great "mass of manuscript materials" gathered through the years. Again, however, Spencer devotes much of this section to the description of routine daily events (at one point quoting passages directly from a diary that he had begun to keep at this time), as well as excursions, social calls, and the like, to show, as he explains, that his life is like any other (2:384). Spencer also records the beginning of his first draft of the *Autobiography* during this period and subsequent references to this project give the final sections of Spencer's self-history an increased sense of process. Spencer's *Data of Ethics* was published in 1879, and in discussing the critical response, Spencer for the first time in the book records his satisfaction with one of the reviews (2:381).

Part 11, which concludes Spencer's narrative in the present time of 1889, on his sixty-ninth birthday, begins with another travelogue, this time based on a journey to Egypt. Spencer then describes the unhappy ending of his massive *Descriptive Sociology* compilation, which failed to generate the interest and sales that it deserved, though he went on to publish an additional volume in his *Principles of Sociology* series and various journal articles. His active involvement in an antiwar and anticolonialism movement in 1881 had "disastrous" effects for his fragile health. He was able to tour America (at the invitation of his American admirers) the next year, but his health suffered yet another setback, and increasingly he lived the life of an invalid. The last paragraphs describe the excruciatingly slow process of composing his autobiography (the equivalent of fifteen printed lines per day), a process that has been nearly his "sole occupation" for the past three years (2:485). As he concludes, parts 2–4, covering the ages seventeen to twenty-eight, during which time he worked as a civil engineer, are still in rough outline form. But he will perhaps conserve the precious little energy he retains for a continuation of his *Principles of Ethics* and finish his autobiography only when he finds it "impracticable to do anything else" (2:486).

Spencer's version of the Augustinian coda, a long essay entitled "Reflections" written in 1893, constitutes the twelfth and final part of the book. Even in the midst of this summing up, consisting largely of self-analysis and his mature philosophical observations on life, he declares his intention to work on further volumes of the *Principles of Sociology*, driven by the need "to fill up a gap in my work" (2:527).

Spencer's conclusion is relatively open-ended, then, emphasizing the process of composition that will end only with total physical disability. As a whole, his autobiographical narrative has a curious form, but in some respects it is much like that of others. Spencer is born with certain innate characteristics that in retrospect make his fate seem inevitable, but they are developed through a series of sometimes chance events that create turning points in his life story. Although Spencer's narrative contains no turning point as dramatic as Darwin's voyage on the *Beagle*, in this respect his autobiography is somewhat similar to Darwin's. Like Mill, he undergoes an unorthodox and eccentric education during his formative years. Like most other autobiographers, he reaches a point in his career at which his major ideas have been developed and the remainder of his career is to be spent in elaborating and applying them. Spencer's outline for his "System of Philosophy," written in his late thirties and given near the beginning of the second volume, although it will be revised, projects virtually all of his future work. Perhaps ironically, this positivist philosopher's self-history is in some ways the ultimate Victorian literary autobiography, portraying a man whose sense of selfhood through most of his adult life is almost totally bound by his publications and the ideas they incorporate, squarely in the tradition of Gibbon's autobiography.

Spencer's autobiography is also a study in extremes and paradox. Spencer calls it a "natural history," a term that is consistent with his naturalist, positivist philosophy. It is appropriate then that the book documents the events it records, and Spencer's autobiography is probably the most highly documented Victorian autobiography— principally relying on correspondence. Spencer as narrator leans so heavily on sources such as letters to his father and, later, to his close friend Lott that at times the narrative consists almost entirely of letters strung together (to use Spencer's own phrase), a method analogous to the compilation of facts in Spencer's philosophical works, most strikingly in his *Descriptive Sociology*. In fact, unlike Newman, who uses documents selectively to narrate crucial actions and states of mind at particular times, Spencer seems to document anything and everything, including the most mundane events in his life, the most extreme example being his quotation of entire pages from his diary to illustrate his daily routine at a certain stage of life.

Insight into the composition process and the situation of the author may help the reader to account for these characteristics of the text: an enfeebled man with the most fragile health and nervous disposition is capable of writing (or rather dictating) for only a few precious minutes at a time during carefully orchestrated routines, choosing to quote letters instead of paraphrasing them or using them as a source, and thus conserving precious time and mental energy. That is, one might make the same sort of allowances that one makes for the unstable Ruskin. However, taken on its own terms, the text is both tedious and eerie in its reliance on documentation. Time and time again, throughout the work, Spencer as narrator notes that the documents supply details that he has entirely forgotten or that they contradict his recollection of the facts. Sometimes the forgotten details are relatively significant, such as the nature of important engineering projects in which he was involved and his initial reaction to

Darwin's *Origin of Species*. While nearly all Victorian autobiographers make at least passing references to the limits of memory, Spencer emphasizes these limits as a refrain throughout the book (though on a few occasions he insists on an important point based solely on his memory).

However disconcerting some readers may find this feature of Spencer's narrative,[5] it is at least compatible with the controlling idea of an objectified, scientific account—that is, a natural history. Paradoxically, however, when the narrator pauses to summarize and interpret his story, he focuses exclusively on a mental development or movement of mind (in the sense that Mill uses the concept) and the succession of publications that incorporate and document that movement. It is true that publication dates can be neatly accommodated by Spencer's remarkably strict chronological narrative structure, one that ties the narrative to historical time more completely than that of any other major Victorian autobiography, each chapter identified by the specific years covered and Spencer's age at the time. However, the series of plot functions that constitute the plot of the protagonist's mental development corresponds to Spencer's universal theory of development and has a decidedly archetypal quality that transcends the chronological organization of the book. The paradox of the narrative is that of Spencer's life and career. He is, after all, a positivist philosopher with admittedly poor powers of observation—a trait consistent with his poor memory. Spencer's genius is not in gathering specific facts but in dealing with abstractions—the most generalized movements of the animate and inanimate world.

Spencer makes the traditional gesture of stating that he is writing frankly, initially for an audience of good friends, for the public only *ex morte,* and, though his chief rhetorical purpose seems to be the public defense and explanation of his works, he also wants to present himself as an ordinary person with ordinary concerns. Although he maintains a good deal of the typical Victorian reticence, he explains his decision not to marry and includes a great deal of personal anecdote and reminiscence. His disclosure of financial troubles and, in particular, his health problems, perhaps intended to elicit sympathy, unfortunately projects a tone of self-pity and a strong hypochondriacal tendency (however real his suffering may have been) and exceeds the limits imposed by most Victorian autobiographers.

Aside from the basic stance of explaining his ideas and works to a public that has from his point of view almost perversely refused to understand or appreciate them properly, Spencer deals specifically with at least two very sensitive aspects of his career. First, he must set the record straight on his debt to Comte—to him, largely a misperception based on coincidence of terminology (sociology, "social statics") and the superficial resemblance of some of their ideas. He is especially careful to deny an early acquaintance with Comte's works and asserts repeatedly that he never shared his friend Mary Ann Evans's enthusiasm for the French thinker, citing his fundamental disagreement with Comte's interpretation of the stages of man's history and his especial dislike of the "religion of mankind."[6]

The other issue has to do with the relationship of his ideas to those of Darwin. Spencer is careful to document the genesis of his "development hypothesis" and his own use of the term *evolution*. He is particularly sensitive to the widely held impression that his talent for synthesis is not matched by a like talent for analysis. Perhaps most importantly, he wants to encourage a historical view that sees Darwin's contribution as reinforcing and validating one aspect of Spencer's overall system of philosophy rather than one that sees Spencer's hypotheses as mere adumbrations of Darwin's theories. Spencer offers generous praise of Darwin's work, but certain references suggest underlying tension and ambivalence. Printing a letter in which he differs with Darwin's ideas on musical expression is certainly in character (2:279), and even Spencer's failure of memory when he tries to recall his original reaction to *Origin of Species* is only one of several striking lapses. However, there is a passage in which Spencer refers to a note of acknowledgment written by Darwin after he had received a copy of Spencer's *Essays* (1857), a note in which Darwin strongly compliments Spencer's ideas. In a remarkable feint, Spencer first offers to quote from the letter, then decides against it, because "the reproduction of it would be out of taste" (2:33).[7] Spencer goes on to reflect upon the autobiographer's dilemma in deciding whether to include "incidents implying success." In attempting to avoid the appearance of vanity, the autobiographer may produce "irremediable distortions" (2:33).

In spite of problems in tone resulting from such defensiveness, from his irritability, and from his hypochondria, Spencer conveys a deep commitment to ideas and to a moral vision much like Mill's,[8] focused on the progress of mankind. Proud of his individuality, eccentricity, and tendency to criticize everything and everyone, he nevertheless values a continued openness to experience and the formation of new ideas (a quality he praises in his father), and the latter sections of the *Autobiography* even imply a certain mellowing in his outlook, even if this quality is concurrent with an increasing pessimism about the future of the world. In his closing chapter, "Reflections," he reaffirms his extremist physiological interpretation of human experience and yet ends in a sort of "return upon himself," to adopt the phrase of Matthew Arnold, as he acknowledges the vast mystery of the universe that drives men to take refuge in "authoritative dogma" (2:549).

The division between author-narrator and protagonist in Spencer's *Autobiography* in one sense is striking. The frequent lapses of memory that cause the narrator to depend on documentary evidence to an extraordinary extent and omit references to periods of life when this evidence is not available, coupled with references to contradiction between this evidence and apparently false memories, consistently reinforce the impression that the narrator is dealing with another person, constructing a biography based on disinterested research rather than an autobiography based primarily on memory.

This fundamental irony is undercut, however, by a very strong, pervasive sense of selfhood that is linked to history in only a vague way—a sense of selfhood identified with well-defined character traits and a powerful and unambiguous narrative of mental development. These characteristics serve to validate origins and enable the narrator to identify closely with the protagonist—even as a child—however spotty the record of memory may be. The well-defined character traits act as a constant in much the same way as those of Ruskin and Darwin do in their autobiographies: Spencer's nonconformity and drive to hypothesize about natural causes, Ruskin's powers of analysis and observation, Darwin's obsessive "grinding" of general laws out of bodies of facts. Spencer's work is more like Mill's, Martineau's, and Darwin's than Ruskin's, of course, in its incorporation of a theoretically informed narrative of personal development.

In spite of Spencer's continuous emphasis on the loss of past time, many anecdotes, vignettes, and scenes from childhood on are incorporated into the book. It could be argued that Spencer's unusually strong emphasis on loss of memory is primarily a product of his narrative method. There seems to be no sure principle of inclusion or exclusion of events in this "natural history." It is as though Spencer wants to tell everything about a particular year or segment of his life. The development-of-mind narrative scheme, however strongly articulated at certain points in the book and however forcefully it defines the destiny of the protagonist and the book's hermeneutics, exerts only a loose control over the myriad of details incorporated into the story. Because of the extensive metadiscourse involved in quoting documents and the frequent references to gaps in the historical record, however, there is a very strong sense of present (reading) time and a correspondingly weak sense of past time.

Spencer's individualism does not prevent him from expressing a strong sense of family continuity, and he not only identifies with the nonconformism inherited from the paternal and maternal sides of his family (though his mother herself seemed to be an exception) but reveals a particularly close father-son relationship. Despite his candid manner of criticizing his father's strengths and weaknesses—the same self-consciously frank manner he uses in criticizing all subjects—the intimate bond between this only child and his father is clear and is not much clouded by resentment or regret, though he does criticize his father for poor treatment of the mother. Spencer, unlike Mill, recalls his mother with affection but, like Mill, credits her with little influence on his life. Among Spencer's evolutionary notions is the (Lamarckian) inheritance of acquired characteristics, so that he explains his own small hands by referring to the teaching profession of both his father and grandfather, one that required little manual labor (2:515–18)! More convincing is the influence of his father's (and, to some extent, his uncles') intellectual curiosity and eccentric views of the world.

A strong sense of isolation is conveyed in the book. Spencer's earliest childhood memory is one of being left alone in a locked house, listening to the peal of church bells, a sound that for many years afterwards brought tears to his eyes (1:73). A sense of pathos arises from the account of increasing isolation by this bachelor and only child after the death of his parents. Finally, his fragile nerves lead to another sort of forced isolation, strictly limiting social intercourse. (He even wears earplugs to avoid hearing idle chatter.) In addition to his "marriage" to his work as a writer and resulting "vow of poverty," self-defined personality traits such as lack of tact, a generally hypercritical attitude, and severe standards of beauty in women interfere with his relationships with women and make marriage impracticable.

Opposed to this sense of isolation, however, is a strong need for, and satisfaction in, friendship. If the irascible, eccentric, and intellectual Spencer seeks to demonstrate the normality of his life by recording his social calls, home visits, and excursions with friends, he is somewhat successful (however much he may bore the reader). Spencer does convey a genuine affection for his closest friends, especially Edward Lott, who, though he married and established a family, remained Spencer's intimate associate, traveling companion, and correspondent for much of his life and accompanied him on his American journey of 1882. Spencer's association with the Smith and Potter families is also important to his life, and his long-standing friendship with fellow intellectuals such as T. H. Huxley, George H. Lewes, and, especially Mary Ann Evans, is well known. Spencer also convincingly reports that he regretted the absence of brothers and, especially, sisters, that he enjoyed living with a family, and that (like so many other Victorian men of letters) he particularly treasured the company of young girls.

The social dimensions of Spencer's life, like his interests in natural scenery and mechanical objects, are tied to the autobiography's enormous surface clutter of detail. When the narrator Spencer pauses to recapitulate and summarize the essential plot functions that give meaning to his story, the reader is left with Spencer and the Universe. Victorian autobiographies tend to deal with universal themes, but Spencer is the ultimate system builder who wants to discover the fundamental laws that explain how everything works. In his "Reflections," in a move reminiscent of Darwin's, he at one point laments the obsession for system building that has so tyrannized his life (2:531), but like the religious prophet who submits himself to God, Spencer, for the most part, submits willingly to his bondage. The theory of development that explains the flow of all things, animate and inanimate, explains Spencer's own life and, by implication, all individual lives, explains the development of his nation and his society, explains the development of world civilization. However, the tension in autobiographical form between surface multiplicity and underlying unity of narrative development is analogous to a fundamental tension in Spencer's thought. He embraces an organic model that predicts ever greater complexity and homogeneity, implies control of all parts of the body by the brain—though the *mind* is "only as deep as the viscera" (2:499) and "pure reason" is a myth—and, by extension, suggests an authoritarian collectivism in social systems. Spencer, however, was emotionally and politically committed to pluralism and radical liberalism, and this unresolved conflict between theoretical models is inseparable from the man who wrote this ultimate life-and-career autobiography.

Chapter 10

Edmund Gosse, *Father and Son* (1907)

Gosse was an eminent if somewhat controversial literary figure in his day and published more than twenty volumes of poetry, biography, and criticism. Today, he is remembered principally for introducing Ibsen and modern Scandinavian literature in general to the English public, but the autobiography *Father and Son* is his only work that is still widely read. His critical works are sometimes derivative and marred by careless scholarship, but Gosse molded his recollections of childhood into one of the classic Victorian autobiographies. He published *Father and Son* when he was fifty-seven.[1]

> The author has observed that those who have written about the facts of their own childhood have usually delayed to note them down until age has dimmed their recollections. Perhaps an even more common fact in such autobiographies is that they are sentimental, and are falsified by self-admiration and self-pity. The writer of these recollections has thought that if the examination of his earliest years was to be undertaken at all, it should be attempted while his memory is still perfectly vivid and while he is still unbiased by the forgetfulness or the sensibility of advancing years. (5)

Like Newman's *Apologia*, *Father and Son* has a problematical status as an autobiography. It certainly is not a full life-and-career autobiography, since it treats the author's life only up to the age of seventeen or so. Gosse thus does not discuss his literary career nor his publications—even Ruskin at least mentions his early publications in *Praeterita*. Then the book has some of the common attributes of fiction, including an economical, relatively fast-paced plot and sharply conceived scenes with considerable dialogue that could hardly be reproduced accurately from the author's memory. Some readers and critics consider the work to be a novel.[2] Even Gosse rejects the term autobiography (212), though he certainly did not think he was writing a novel.

Nevertheless, *Father and Son* is widely read and studied as an autobiography, and for obvious reasons. To begin, Gosse's statement of purpose and his contract with the reader is typical of Victorian autobiography. He claims that his narrative is "scrupulously true" and specifically contrasts it with the "ingenious" and "specious" fiction of his day. The only "tampering with precise fact" has been to alter the names of many of the persons mentioned in the book (5–6).[3] The narrative is offered to the public "as a *document*, as a record of past educational and religious conditions" and the "diagnosis of a dying Puritanism." In a subsidiary sense, it offers "a study of the development of moral and intellectual ideas during the progress of infancy" (5). Like other Victorian autobiographers, Gosse presents his story as a true, factual personal history that can be integrated into the larger history of the age. Contributing to this sense is the fact that the father Philip Gosse was a botanist of some note with a historical significance of his own. Much like Mill, Gosse is offering himself as a case study that will help to explain the immediately preceding age to contemporary readers. Like Newman, he intentionally records only a fragment of his life, but one that traces an unconversion rather than a conversion experience and deals with childhood rather than adulthood.

Gosse himself apparently rejects the term autobiography because he is writing the history of the relationship between himself and his father rather than a self-history in the strict sense. However, the narrative necessarily focuses on Gosse rather than his father, despite the consistent attempt to analyze and explain the latter's thoughts and feelings. The reason is simple: it is the son who is developing, growing. He is the protagonist of the story. The father, with his genuine but suffocating love and the fanatical, religious worldview that dominated his own life and stifled that of his son, acts as a foil to the son who grows ever more conscious of his selfhood and of his aversion to his father's ideas. To be sure, the father's life contains dramatic incidents—his wife's death, the terrible shock to his career brought on by the theory of evolution and his ill-conceived book *Omphalos*,[4] his remarriage, his struggle to control the life of his son.

However, his philosophy of life remains a constant, while the principal narrative movement is based on the son's mental development. In fact, there are two levels in the narrative, the external world of the Gosse household, practically a little universe unto itself, and the internal world of the son's mind. The most dynamic events are the internal, mental events. They provide the principal functions of the plot. The father dominates the action in the external world but is unaware of the internal events in the son's mind until their narrative breaks into the open and disrupts the relationship between father and son. The open-ended conclusion of the narrative suggests that from this point on, the son's internal life story will merge with, or perhaps dominate, that of his external life.

In spite of Gosse's limiting thesis and his focus on the father-son relationship, it is clear that the son's very essence of selfhood, not just some part of it, is in question here. In fact, rather than classifying the story strictly as that of a father-son relationship, it is more accurate to say that Gosse is struggling for self-expression against a confining environment dominated at first (up to the age of eight) by both his mother and father (perhaps the mother is the more imposing and forceful figure) and then after the mother's death by the father himself, at least partially in conformance to the mother's plans for her son. One could carry this argument further and say that Gosse conceives of his inner struggle as being directed against an abstract force, that is, a certain kind of religious fanaticism that holds both mother and father in its grip and has in fact stifled their lives as well by imprisoning their own artistic inclinations. (The mother had a natural gift for poetic expression, the father for drawing and painting). However, at the highest level of abstraction, as Gosse himself claims, his book "is the record of a struggle between . . . two epochs" (9).

Gosse's narrative consists of twelve untitled chapters and an epilogue. The organization is strictly chronological. After an introductory chapter in which he outlines his purpose and, making use of his father's and mother's diaries, reconstructs portraits of his parents and their relationship at the time of his birth (he was "given . . . to the Lord"), he begins the second chapter with his earliest memories of childhood. As an only child, Gosse lived a quiet life with his father and mother, dominated by religious observance; however, a "series of minute and soundless incidents," beginning as early as age six, initiate the internal story of his mental development, as inherent features, independent of his training or environment, begin to assert themselves (32). This "instinctive" life, developing "unexpectedly," came to be associated with nature, beauty, and art, as well as a kind of "natural magic" that the son invents in his own mind to parallel the religion of his parents (38). The first "shocks" that led to this awakening of consciousness came from apparently trifling incidents in family life that suggest that his father is not omniscient, like God (33–34).

At the age of seven, during the time he watched his mother suffer from the sickness that would soon kill her, Gosse by chance came upon an obscure pious poem called "The Cameronian's Dream" that gave him his first taste of "nature-romance" (53).

The mother's suffering prior to her death, when he was eight, was eased somewhat by the thought that her son had been "dedicated" to God. After her death, the son led the "healthy life" of an "ordinary little boy" for a brief time, an experience that made him more curious about human life (71), but he soon entered into a close and confining life with his father. He learned to share his father's attitudes, such as his intense anti-Catholicism, but was already "secretly hostile" to certain Evangelical hymns and enjoyed parts of the New Testament for their "literary" effect (73).

A move with his father to the Devonshire sea coast in his ninth year introduced into his life a Wordsworthian love of the sea (81). However, his father's troubles with Darwinism and his own ill health and ill temper brought misery to their lives. The son continued to develop his appreciation for natural beauty; on the other hand, the father strengthened their ties with a local group of "Saints" and began to preach. The son learned the discipline of work by imitating the writing and art work of his botanist father. At the age of ten, he was allowed to develop a friendship with a child of his own age. About the same time, he discovered a "miracle" while studying Virgil (the least objectional of the classical poets from an Evangelical point of view): the "incalculable, the amazing beauty which could exist in the sound of verses" (131).

In spite of an increased religious commitment and a public baptism at the instigation of his father ("the central act of my childhood"), the son's self-consciousness remained intact and led to increased secrecy from his father (158). At the age of eleven, he was permitted to read *Tom Cringle's Log* and "discovered" prose. Reading "fortified his individuality" more than anything else (161). He began to attend a local school, and at the suggestion of the retired playwright Sheridan Knowles, who lived in the vicinity, he read Shakespeare—until his father put a stop to the practice.

His father's remarriage (to a woman somewhat sympathetic to the son's interests) opened up a more tolerant period; he was allowed to read Dickens's *Pickwick Papers* and began to understand painting. The son continued to love and admire his father but became more critical of his views and rebelled against him in subtle ways. His introduction to Greek art through engravings at the age of thirteen led him to entertain the "dangerous and pagan notion that beauty palliates evil" (199). The son felt increasingly alienated from the group of fanatical "Saints" with whom he and his father were associated.

After being sent to boarding school, the son drifted even further from his father, who eventually was compelled to give up the "Great Scheme" of his son's total dedication to the "service of the Lord." Boarding school, however, was boring, and the son did not make friends there. Nevertheless, he was "pursuing certain lines of moral and mental development all the time" (215). He was not "consciously in any revolt" against his strict religious faith, but he was increasingly aware of the underlying conflict between that faith and his growing appreciation for literature. He carried in his head a strange mixture of *Endymion* and the Book of Revelation, John Wesley's hymns and *Midsummer Night's Dream*.

The son's personal religious crisis came when, at the age of seventeen, he prepared to leave home to live in London. His intense prayer for Christ to take him to Paradise (an echo of his father's apocalyptic hopes) ended in the Clough-like reflection that "[t]he Lord has not come, the Lord will never come." From that moment, "my Father and I, though the fact was long successfully concealed from him and even from myself, walked in opposite hemispheres of the soul, with 'the thick o' the world between us'" (232).

Thus ends the narrative proper, but Gosse immediately continues in an epilogue: "This narrative ... must not be allowed to close with the son in the foreground of the piece" (233). It is as though the narrator is resisting the inevitable tendency of his story to become essentially a self-history of mental development, rather than the story of a relationship.[5] He goes on to record the anguish of both father and son during the following four years as the father attempts to maintain his control over the son's religious life (which is understood to be at the center of his identity) through frequent correspondence and close questioning during his visits home. A definitive confrontation during one of these visits is followed by a pathetic letter from the father expressing his disappointment and hope for reconciliation but offering no hope for compromise in his rigid religious position. The book closes in this way:

> No compromise... would have been acceptable... and thus desperately challenged, the young man's conscience threw off once for all the yoke of his "dedication," and, as respectfully as he could, without parade or remonstrance, he took a human being's privilege to fashion his inner life for himself. (250)

Once again, the story ends with the son's mental development, this time after a definitive break with the father. Like other Victorian autobiographies, *Father and Son* tells a story of self-development, though with a novelistic neatness. In fact, the epilogue, rather than correcting the too great emphasis on the son's development, as the narrator Gosse apparently intends, reinforces the formal sense of completeness and closure in the son's story, since it takes him up to his twenty-first year, the year of his majority, as it establishes the fact of his psychological independence and adulthood.

Although *Father and Son* is not a literary autobiography in the sense of portraying Gosse's career as a writer, its plot structure obviously can be described as a syntagm of plot functions corresponding to the first section or sections, "Childhood" and "Youth," of the conventional literary life and career. The series of plot functions defined by the mostly internal events seems to lead inevitably to the final one—the break with the father, the independent career. Furthermore, though Gosse does not mention the specific nature of his new career, each plot function reinforces the seemingly innate tendency toward art, literature, and the love of beauty that will underlie that career. The aesthetic sense, built up in opposition to the static, confining religiosity of his parents, is at the center of Gosse's new self-identity at the end of the book.

For Gosse this aesthetic sense, incorporating a sort of Swinburnian, paganistic love of natural beauty, is closely allied with the concept of scientific progress. Despite his scientific training, the father is unable to let go of his fundamentalist belief system in order to accept the fossil evidence of continual change. The instinctive strategy of the protagonist, enabled by his developing subjective dualism and interior dialogue, is to retreat to a "savage," more primitive religion, at least as an intellectual exercise, and then, retaining his momentum, quickly work through his father's version of Christianity to a positivistic acceptance of intellectual progress while retaining his aesthetic sensibility. He seems to spontaneously devise for himself a course of development that will bring him in line with the major intellectual and cultural movements of his age, much as they were defined by Mill.

There are, however, underlying uncertainties and contradictions in this scheme so clearly articulated in the narrator's thematic statements. For example, as Cynthia Northcutt Malone has pointed out in a recent study, Gosse acknowledges that the breathtakingly beautiful "fairy paradise" of the Devonshire tidal pools where he once helped his father collect marine specimens has been destroyed by the "idle-minded curiosity" of visitors who have been inspired by his father's books on the subject, his "most valuable contribution" to genuine scientific knowledge. Malone relates the idea of the destructive consequences of scientific progress to the loss of Gosse's childhood world dominated by his parents as it recedes ever further into the past.[6]

The precision or neatness of Gosse's plot is partially the product of his thematic control (as in Newman's *Apologia*) but it is also a product of Gosse's confined and limited childhood life. For the same reasons the narrative generates well-defined paradigmatic oppositions.

The thesis of Gosse the narrator has already been noted, and in the epilogue he forcefully reiterates it: "Let me speak plainly. After my long experience . . . I surely have the right to protest against the untruth . . . that evangelical religion, or any religion in a violent form, is a wholesome or valuable or desirable adjunct to human life." After a long list of its destructive and divisive effects, he writes, "There is something horrible . . . in the fanaticism that can do nothing with this pathetic and fugitive existence of ours but treat it as if it were the uncomfortable ante-chamber to a palace which no one has explored and of the plan of which we know absolutely nothing" (246–47).[7]

The rhetorical effectiveness of *Father and Son* is largely a product of the narrator's ability to convey a real affection and sympathy for his father (and mother) apart from his outrage at the oppressive religion that dominated their lives, that in fact kept them from realizing their own artistic and intellectual potential. In addition, Gosse's serious theme does not prohibit his including the sort of nostalgic, entertaining, and humorous anecdotes typical of Victorian childhood memories: investigating the wonderful world of the sea pools along the Devonshire coast with his father, experiencing the solemn and absurd ritual of baptism among the Saints, naively reciting a poem with objectionable words and images to a shocked "polite company." Gosse's tone throughout is that of a sophisticated but sympathetic adult speaking to the English public, stressing his awareness of developing social norms and the historical significance of his message, refraining from self-pity in his most personal references.

The distance between narrator and protagonist is relatively great, since, through most of the story, the boy is not aware of the significance of the growth process that is taking place in his mind. This in itself is not an unusual characteristic of Victorian autobiography, but Gosse foregrounds the young protagonist's lack of understanding. In retrospect, the narrator interprets the boy's dream about the color carmine (122), analyzes his lack of appreciation for Bible reading (238), and so on. This distance of course enables Gosse the narrator to represent emotional, even heart-rending scenes with a rhetorical objectivity. Finally, because the narrator leaves his protagonist at the threshold of his adult career, the protagonist never fully develops into the mature writer who narrates the story.

Thus, the present time of the book is clearly demarcated from the past time of the story. The vision of time past is very clear, however. Gosse documents his story by quoting from the diaries of both mother and father early on and from his father's correspondence toward the end; nevertheless, this documentation seems to be cited primarily because of its intrinsic interest or even for dramatic effect rather than to compensate for an unreliable memory. Although Gosse occasionally refers to the limits of his memory, he does not foreground those limits. He seems to have a remarkably good memory for specific incidents from his childhood and dramatizes them as if they were scenes from a play. The sharp definition of past time is significant on two levels. It helps Gosse attain the objective distance that he seeks in describing highly emotional scenes and states of mind. In this sense, it helps to build dramatic irony. For instance, the unalloyed joy that the father felt on the occasion of his son's baptism and apparent conversion seems "pathetic" to the author-narrator and his implied reader in the present time of the book (150). On another level, the demarcation of past time helps to establish the book itself as a historical document, an effect that is consistent with Gosse's intentions, as he explains in the preface. The father belonged to an earlier generation, an earlier age that *we*, the narrator and the implied reader, who belong to a later generation, a later age, can now place in historical perspective. And there can be no doubt that the present age is relatively enlightened, released from the grip of a benighted religious tradition. The book as a whole argues for a strongly progressive view of social history.

Gosse's long childhood journey into consciousness and enlightenment, then, corresponds to the general movement of society. His self-history is a particularly extreme individual example of a general development within English history. Unlike Matthew Arnold, who wanders between two worlds in his poem "The Grande Chartreuse," the narrator Gosse believes that he belongs to a new zeitgeist, a dynamic present that is fast leaving behind the "dying Puritanism" of Philip Gosse. But balanced against a contempt for that old "horrible . . . fanaticism" of his parents is a sense of loss—of a youthful, mythic time of unity and certainty, dominated by the vivid father and ghostly mother portrayed in the text.

Chapter 11

Francis Galton, *Memories of My Life* (1908)

Francis Galton's autobiography, published three years before his death,[1] is of considerable interest as a historical document. Galton, who shared a famous grandfather (Erasmus Darwin) with Charles Darwin, was acquainted with many important Victorian figures—in particular, scientists and explorers—and he filled his book with descriptions of them and anecdotes about them. Galton was himself an explorer of note, with pioneering mapping expeditions to the Near East and South Africa to his credit, and he also made contributions to meteorology, the use of fingerprinting to establish identity, correlation theory in statistics, composite photographic portraiture, the functioning of visual memory, and other scientific and technical areas.

However, the image of the precocious Galton as a Victorian genius deeply involved in a great age of discovery and advancement has been eclipsed in large measure by a more ominous image associated with his work in inheritance theory and his enthusiastic promotion of eugenics (a word he coined). Because Galton used the latter chapters of *Memories* to argue his case for eugenics, the book itself for many modern readers illustrates only too well a dark side to Victorian culture. Galton seems remarkably smug in his views of genetic hierarchies and insensitive to the moral and political issues raised by the concept of genetic engineering.

In his preface, Galton informs the reader that his "'Memories' are arranged under the subjects to which they refer, and only partially in chronological order" (v). Nevertheless, the first half of the book, roughly speaking, is cast in a fairly consistent chronological narrative, with an implicit theme of personal development.

Galton's opening chapters on "Parentage" and "Childhood and Boyhood," as their titles suggest, represent a conventional beginning of the life-and-career autobiography. The only unusual feature is Galton's tight organization, systematically identifying grandparents, parents, brothers and sisters and quickly summarizing his early education at schools in Boulogne, Kenilworth, and Birmingham (King Edward's "Free School"). From his progenitors, he has inherited "a considerable taste for science, for poetry, and for statistics; also . . . a rather unusual power of enduring physical fatigue without harmful results" but, unfortunately, also a susceptibility toward bronchitis and asthma (11). As for the schools, the French one was poor and ineffective and the "literary provender" provided by Dr. Jeune at Birmingham was unsuitable to young Galton's mind. However, he "owes much to [the] influence of Mr. Atwood, who kept the school at Kenilworth."

In the third chapter, "Medical Studies," the narrator comes closest to establishing a strong narrative momentum in telling a story of development. Because of his parents' wishes and his natural abilities, the young protagonist was intended for the medical profession. His first experience in this line, at the age of sixteen, was to observe a doctor's postmortem examination. In 1838, he began to study with enthusiasm at Birmingham General Hospital. Much of the chapter is taken up by anecdotes concerning his stay there, and the narrator's continuing speculation concerning hysteria, delirium tremens, and other illnesses and conditions. After several months at the hospital, Galton was sent to spend a pleasant year of medical studies under Professor Richard Partridge at King's College. In the final paragraph of the chapter, Galton skims over the remaining five years of his medical studies. He attended lectures at Cambridge and studied for a short time at St. George's Hospital. Then his father died, and "the direction of my life became changed" (47).

In the midst of relating his experience at the Birmingham hospital, Galton writes,

> There were many incidents that I could tell about this time of my life that might be interesting in some sense, but which are foreign to the main purpose of such an autobiography as mine, which is to indicate how the growth of a mind has been affected by circumstances. I will, however, make one exception, which refers to a very narrow escape from drowning. (45)

Galton's statement of purpose seems to indicate a design such as Mill's, but the subsequent anecdote about his near drowning is far from the last of its kind. In fact, though Galton follows a roughly chronological structure for the next few chapters until he finally adopts a topical arrangement, the text is primarily made up of reminiscences, memoirs, and travelogues. Two observations are pertinent here. First, the death of Galton's father made him independently wealthy and thus not dependent on a medical career, which he then gave up. Therefore, the budding "career" in its strict sense, linked to his unified mental development, was abandoned, and Galton was free to follow various lines of thought and action. Second, on a deeper level, Galton's purported scheme of showing mental growth as affected by *circumstances* seems to clash with the genetic model that Galton the protagonist developed later in his career and upon which Galton the narrator focuses more and more in the later chapters of the book. In other words, the concept of genetic inheritance seems to imply a preordained mental development or unfolding (reminiscent of Ruskin's version of himself) rather than a development formed by environmental influences.

Chapter 4, "Short Tour to the East," is a brief travelogue describing a tour that took him to central Europe and the Middle East just prior to his Cambridge years. However, his introductory sentence—"In the spring of 1840 a passion for travel seized me as if I had been a migrating bird"—introduces the theme of travel and exploration that is going to figure significantly in the story of his life. The journey "vastly widened my views of humanity and civilization, and it confirmed aspirations for travel which were afterwards indulged" (57).

The fifth chapter is devoted to his university career at Cambridge and is full of details about Trinity College and his teachers and fellow students, many of whom were prominent Englishmen. Galton justifies his method in this way: "A main object of giving the foregoing brief notices of notable persons with whom I had the privilege of being acquainted at Cambridge, is to show the enormous advantages offered by a University to those who care to profit by them" (80). Aside from indicating the process of socialization by which Galton was becoming part of an elite group, this chapter is also important for its reference to his "utter breakdown" in health during his third year at Cambridge (a sign of things to come) and to his father's death in 1844. As already noted, this event caused Galton to give up his intention to enter the medical profession, so that his "status of pupilhood was closed" (82). But the death of the powerful and influential father had other effects on Galton's personal life. His death removed "the main bond that kept our family together, and we soon became more or less separated" (82). This is the most significant turning point of the story, suddenly giving Galton personal independence and status in society. He was eager to "sow his wild oats" in travel (85).

The following two chapters treat Galton's subsequent expeditions to Egypt and the Sudan and to Syria, undertaken in 1845, when he was twenty-three years old. Galton's anecdotes about his interesting and often dangerous adventures in exotic lands—including a journey to Khartoum—are spiced with short sketches of the characters he met along the way, not only Muslim government officials and chieftains, but displaced eccentrics such as Mansfield Parkyns, a Cambridge friend who had left school prematurely after a "scrape," and Arnaud Bey, a distinguished St. Simonian who had been banished from France. Galton the narrator defends his travelogue:

> My excuses for speaking at such length about countries since so familiarly known are that it will help to give some idea of how they struck a tourist-traveller in the time of Mehemet Ali, upwards of sixty years ago, and because this little excursion formed one of the principal landmarks of my life. That chance meeting with Arnaud Bey had important after-results to me by suggesting scientific objects to my future wanderings. (97)

That is, the sower of wild oats was going to adopt increasingly the role of scientific explorer in his future expeditions. Galton ends this two-chapter account of his journey very neatly by describing the deaths of his two pet monkeys, who had accompanied him most of the way, soon after he returned to England.

Upon his return to Clarendon to visit his mother and sister, it occurred to Galton that he was

> ignorant of the very ABC of the life of a country gentleman, such as most of the friends of my family had been familiar with from childhood. I was totally unused to hunting, and I had no proper

experience of shooting. This deficiency was remedied during the next three or four years. . . . The next year I established myself at Leamington, jobbed horses, and hunted methodically. (110)

The chapter in which Galton describes his methodical self-education as a country gentleman is appropriately entitled "Hunting and Shooting." It covers the years 1846–50. Galton by no means confined himself to the gentlemanly sports of grousing and running foxes, however. With characteristic zeal, he sailed up to the Shetlands, where he spent a summer in seal-shooting—"I would not shoot a seal now, but youths are murderous by instinct, and so was I" (112). An experience in ballooning during this period provides another anecdote (115–18). Galton writes that he was not really intellectually idle during this period, however, for he was reading continuously and thinking seriously about science. His experiments with electricity and the teletype led to a pamphlet in 1849, the first of what was to become a steady stream of publications that continued for the rest of his life.

Chapters 9 and 10 describe Galton's 1850–52 expedition into southeast Africa, undertaken in association with the Royal Geographical Society. Interestingly, Galton the narrator describes two motives for the journey: the scientific zeal to help fill up the "blank spaces in the map of the world" and the desire to hunt big game. Much as Darwin refers to his published *Journal of the Beagle*, Galton refers to the published accounts of his mapping expedition in which a full account has been given. He gives the "bare details" of his journey among the Damaras, Ovampo, and Namaquas; as before, his adventures are fleshed out by anecdotes about exotic customs and dangers from the harsh environment and his savage hosts. In recognition of Galton's contributions to mapping the center of South Africa, a "country hitherto unknown," the Royal Geographical Society awarded him a gold medal in 1854. The award gave him "an established position in the scientific world" and led to other honors, including election to the Royal Society and the Atheneum Club (151).

Shortly after his return to England and a subsequent period of recovery from the ill health he had suffered from the effects of his travels, Galton became engaged to his future wife. His treatment of his married life is altogether typical of Victorian autobiographers.

After a brief statement concerning his right to privacy, he summarizes the contents of his eleventh chapter, "After Return Home—Marriage":

> I shall say little about my purely domestic life, which, however full of interest to myself, would be uninteresting to strangers, so I attempt no more than to give brief accounts of the friendships and events that followed my marriage in 1853 up to about 1866. This interval of thirteen years occupies a fairly well defined part of my life owing to two reasons, namely, that my scientific interest during its latter half became concentrated on heredity, and because it was in 1866 that my health suffered a more serious breakdown than had happened to it before. (154–55)

Galton gives only a very brief description of his own extended family and that of his wife, however, and this chapter is only a few pages in length. Subsequent chapters do not closely follow the 1853–66 outline.

Galton then devotes a short chapter to his book *The Art of Travel* (1855), which enabled him to give other travelers and explorers the benefit of his experience, though he was too ill to take part in further expeditions himself.

A long chapter entitled "Social Life" follows, with dozens of references to friends and acquaintances, many of them writers, scientists, and other well-known figures. Among the many anecdotes are his contribution to the Victorian genre of "Carlyle as Bore" and an amusing description of Herbert Spencer's trip to the Derby. Chapter 14, "Geography and East Africa," is also largely anecdotal. In the course of describing his own interests and activities within the Royal Geographical Society, Galton comments on well-known events such as the controversial expedition by Richard Burton and J. H. Speke in 1856 (planned by Galton himself) which led to the discovery of Lake Victoria and the source of the Nile. He also comments on the legendary exploits of Livingstone and Stanley.

Much in the manner of Besant, who devoted separate chapters to his connections with particular organizations and their projects, Galton goes on to describe his longstanding involvement with the British Association in chapter 15. Galton had to resign as general secretary after his "complete breakdown" in 1866, but as late as 1898 channeled his attempts to methodize the preservation of records for pedigree stock of animals through the association (217). (Again, he was thwarted by ill health.) Galton devotes the closing pages of the chapter to a reminiscence concerning Sir William Grove, who had served as one of the presidents of the association. Then, in another relatively short chapter, Galton relates his activities associated with meteorology at the Kew Observatory. He briefly describes several of his contributions, such as the development of techniques to standardize sextants, rapidly verify thermometers, and "rate" watches, and his original observations concerning cyclones and various "laws of weather." He speculates about the future use of cannon shells to gain knowledge concerning upper air currents and various improvements in meteorological design and methodology.

In chapter 17, Galton discusses his design and use of anthropometric laboratories, a prelude to his exposition of hereditary theory toward the end of the book. Galton's first laboratory was part of the International Exhibition of 1884. For three pence, an applicant could be tested for "Keenness of Sight and of Hearing; Colour Sense; Judgement of Eye; Breathing Power; Reaction Time; Strength of Pull and of Squeeze; Force of Blow; Span of Arms; Height, both standing and sitting; and Weight" (245). Next comes Galton's pioneering work in the use of fingerprinting as a method of identification, which he discusses toward the end of the chapter. Chapter 18 describes Galton's work on composite portraits and stereoscopic maps. Galton was interested in composite portraits both for their application to criminology and for their value in suggesting racial and familial types.

In chapter 19, "Human Faculty," Galton covers his attempts to extend his ideas about human measurement from physical qualities to mental ones and his developing ideas concerning "race improvement."

> After I had become satisfied of the inheritance of all the mental qualities into which I had inquired, and that heredity was a far more powerful agent in human development than nurture, I wished to explore the range of human faculty in various directions in order to ascertain the degree to which breeding might, at least theoretically, modify the human race. (266)

However, this chapter, like the others, is haphazardly organized and largely given to anecdotes and Galton's speculations about unusual or unrecognized mental phenomena.

Most of the events and publications mentioned in chapter 19 had taken place in the 1880s; in the next chapter, "Heredity," Galton goes back to describe the revolutionary effect that the publication in 1859 of Darwin's *Origin of Species* had on his own mental development. "Its effect was to demolish a multitude of dogmatic barriers by a single stroke, and to arouse a spirit of rebellion against all ancient authorities whose positive and unauthenticated statements were contradicted by modern science" (287).

Galton was soon at work applying ideas of heredity to human populations. "I had been immensely impressed by many obvious cases of heredity among the Cambridge men who were at the University about my own time" (288). By 1865, he had published two articles with the combined title "Hereditary Talent and Character" in *Macmillan's Magazine*. These articles contained the germs of future books: *Hereditary Genius* (1869), *English Men of Science* (1874), *Human Faculty* (1883), and *Natural Inheritance* (1889). At this point in the book, Galton's life story merges with his developing bibliography in a manner familiar to Victorian autobiography, though Galton continues to emphasize his ideas rather than the publications themselves. In his research, much of it statistical, he increasingly focused on the "Transmission of Qualities" among the members of a family. Galton goes on to discuss his formulations of the "laws of heredity" in some detail. Like Darwin and other autobiographers who associate sudden flashes of insight with particular detailed scenes, he recalls the moment when he first grasped the generalization that the laws of heredity were based on statistical deviations:[2] "It was in the grounds of Naworth castle. . . . A temporary shower drove me to seek refuge in a reddish recess in the rock. . . . There the idea flashed across me, and I forgot everything else for a moment in my great delight" (300).

The final chapter, "Race Improvement," is Galton's version of the philosophical essay or Augustinian coda that we have seen in several of the other autobiographies. Eugenics had been one of Galton's interests since the 1860s and for the last few years his primary concern. In present, "book" time, he makes his case for that controversial science as being eminently reasonable and even truly philanthropic, and he expresses his hopes for the work being carried on by Professor Karl Pearson (Galton's biographer and something of a disciple) in the Galtonian mode. Galton is also arguing for the consistency and coherence of his ideas, demonstrating by frequent quotations that his early views on race improvement expressed in the 1865 articles, with only slight modifications, are consistent with his present positions.

The autobiographical narrative as a whole, however, does not carry with it a strong sense of continuous development. Galton's early medical interests and training do not lead to the medical profession nor to medical research. His career as explorer begins in sport, and though it leads to long-standing intellectual interests as well as personal prestige and social status, it is not closely related to his subsequent obsession with eugenics, and only obliquely to his meteorological and other subsidiary interests. Galton continually interrupts his developmental plot line by inserting anecdotes, observations, opinions. What is consistent in Galton's narrative is a tireless and irrepressible curiosity about the natural world and man's relationship to it and a commitment to the "improvement" of society or mankind as an ideal.

Galton's rhetorical stance on the most obvious level can be described easily. He is an English gentleman speaking to other English gentlemen of his class. Like his friend Spencer he defends a scientific world view that emphasizes the physical basis of all phenomena and sees himself as a pioneer in establishing a new order based on that view. Unlike Spencer, however, he is a Cambridge man, an insider who has connections with many of the "best" families in England and is proud to count numerous eminent scientists and intellectuals among his friends and associates. He refers to about 260 of them by name.[3] An example: "An early friendship that exercised great influence in shaping my future scientific life was that of General, afterwards Sir Edward, Sabine, R.A., and President of the Royal Society" (224). He goes on to summarize Sabine's career and indicate by the inclusion of his birth and death dates that an entry on him may be found in the *Dictionary of National Biography*. He stresses his kinship with Charles Darwin as well as the compatibility of their work and ideas. Public honors and titles, as well as his publications, are highly significant to him and establish his credentials as a spokesman for English society.

Most emphatically, he argues for the cluster of ideas and attitudes surrounding eugenics, which represents over three decades of his work, the most important work of his life. He purports to see an increasing acceptance of his ideas, which will, after all, save society from the disaster of genetic corruption and decline. Put simply, eugenics naturally follows from, and will supplant, the process of natural selection in human beings. Thus, his role can be aptly termed prophetic.

Like other autobiographers, he also seeks to set the record straight on particular issues. Most important, of course, is his care in demonstrating Darwin's approval and support of his ideas by quoting from his cousin's letters. He also seeks to clarify the nature of his own contributions to science—especially in the application of fingerprinting techniques, as distinct from the work of the Frenchman Alphonse Bertillon. Finally, he clarifies the historical record in other small ways, as in giving the insider's version of the Livingstone-Stanley drama.

Galton's practice of giving the birth and death dates of each person covered by the *Dictionary of National Biography* serves to emphasize the status of his *Memories* as a historical document, especially in such chapters as "Cambridge" and "Social Life," in which Galton seems intent on mentioning as many of these people as possible.

In spite of the smugness and insularity that a modern reader, particularly a non-English one, might encounter in this book so firmly grounded in a particular time and place, there is at least one aspect of the persona shared by narrator and protagonist that makes a wider appeal. Even more than the inventor-engineer-philosopher Spencer, Galton conveys a spontaneous and irrepressible—and sometimes almost boyishly naive—curiosity about the world around him and about human experience. The ultimate dilettante, Galton wants to explore not only darkest Africa but every conceivable aspect of physical and mental phenomena. Aside from the relatively conventional examples involving teletype, weather maps, fingerprinting, and so forth, he cites others that are unusual to say the least, especially his introspective experiments involving abnormal states of mind. On a walk one morning, he began to imagine that everything and everyone he met was a "spy" and found the experiment "only too successful," establishing in himself an "uncanny sensation" that lasted for hours. On another occasion, he succeeded in producing barbarian-like sensations of idolatry in himself by imaginatively investing a comic picture of Punch with divine attributes (276–77). He attempted to verify the existence of mental images of numbers or "Number-Forms" by questioning his colleagues (271–72). At another point, he measured the boredom of people by "counting the number of their Fidgets" (278). In connection with his interest in fostering the "best stock" through eugenics, he contrived to construct a

> "Beauty-Map" of the British Isles. Whenever I have occasion to classify the person I meet into three classes, "good, medium, bad," I use a needle mounted as a pricker, wherewith to prick holes, unseen, in a piece of paper, torn rudely into a cross with a long leg. I use its upper end for "good," the cross arm for "median," and lower end for "bad." The object, place, and date are written on the paper. (315)

Galton found London to rank highest for female beauty, Aberdeen lowest!

There is little distance between narrator and protagonist, in spite of the lost early career in medicine. Galton includes very few memories from his very early childhood; he does not follow through with his implied narrative outline of personal development with any force or consistency. As author-narrator he often injects retrospective speculations about various subjects into his narrative of past events, but he emphasizes the consistency of his ideas respecting eugenics since he began to write about them in the mid-1860s. All these characteristics blunt the distinction between protagonist and narrator. Unlike many autobiographers, most notably Spencer, he does not foreground loss of memory, a practice that always implies a disjunction between book time and past time, between narrator and protagonist.

Galton reinforces this continuity between past and present by describing

> a rather weird effect that compiling these "Memories" has produced on me. By much dwelling upon them they became refurbished and so vivid as to appear as sharp and definite as things of to-day. The consequence has been an occasional obliteration of the sense of Time, and to replace it by the idea of a permanent panorama.

The distinctions among past, present, and future are obliterated in a perpetual "now" (277–78). This observation is of course related to Galton's other speculations about psychic phenomena.

Although he is obviously aware that his promotion of eugenics is very controversial, he does not identify himself as separate from or opposed to either his social or physical environment to nearly the extent that some Victorian autobiographers do. His few references to his father are positive and even reverential. Although he implies a very close father-son relationship, he does not analyze it or trace its course of development. Although he implies that family members drift apart after his father's death, he refers to his mother and sisters (who help to nurse him back to health after his African expedition) only in positive terms, though he gives scant details of domestic life at any point in his life. What he does emphasize is a strong sense of extended family in his own case and, to a lesser extent, in his wife's. This sense of family is of course ultimately connected in his mind with theories concerning family and racial types and, in the largest sense, with eugenics itself.

Galton fits the stereotype of the Victorian gentleman whose hunger for knowledge about the world and its people and in all their diversity is seemingly insatiable and yet who closely identifies himself with his own insular and elitist society. This fundamental irony in his self-image and way of life is also found at the heart of his theoretical views, and indeed Galton, like the other Victorian autobiographers to some degree, expects to be closely identified with the ideas by which he is publicly known and that are documented in the publications he lists in full at the end of his text. Indeed, eugenics implies a universal view of mankind as one part of the physical world that wants management and guidance. The future history of the world depends on the proper channeling of the process that has until now depended upon natural selection. Utopia (full of happy, healthy humanity) or oblivion (brought on by the dominance of the unfit) awaits mankind. Galton as an individual, however, is not only the spokesman for the elite remnant who must impose their rational and justifiable rule upon the earth but he is also a member of their gene pool.[4] On the most obvious level, Galton's ability to quickly "devour" and assimilate Darwin's ideas "may be ascribed to an hereditary bent of mind that both its illustrious author and myself have inherited from our common grandfather, Dr. Erasmus Darwin" (288). A universal vision is finally enclosed in a tribal-nationalist framework, and it is to his fellow members that Galton addresses himself.

Conclusion

Although Victorian autobiographies have been studied by critics and scholars more than ever in recent years, they are often considered ahistorically and compared with autobiographies from other cultures and times; treated together with fiction and poetry as expressions of an impulse or mode; or subdivided into exclusive categories such as spiritual or scientific, *ex morte* or *ex libre*. I have taken a different approach, assuming the autobiography to be a historically defined genre that can accommodate these various modes and subdivisions but one that is distinct from the novel and other genres.

In the course of discussing eleven Victorian autobiographies successively in chronological order, I have suggested formal and conventional continuities among them. In this concluding chapter I will reiterate and discuss some of those continuities, but first let me return to the working definition of autobiography, that of Phillipe Lejeune, given in the introduction: a "[r]etrospective prose narrative written by a real person concerning his own existence, where the focus is his individual life, in particular the story of his personality." According to a rough count of the listings in William Matthews's bibliography of British autobiographies,[1] about two thousand titles were published in the second half of the nineteenth century. Many of these books are composed largely of war adventures, travelogues, reminiscences about famous friends and acquaintances, and so forth, and many of them probably do not adequately focus on the writer's life and personality to qualify as genuine autobiographies according to Lejeune's definition.[2] More recently, Jerome H. Buckley has pointed out that while only about 23 autobiographical works written by British *literary figures* were on record before 1800, at least 175 such works were published during the nineteenth century.[3]

We should not forget the historical context of text production when we set out to analyze the Victorian autobiography. Like hundreds of other autobiographers, each writer we have studied is certified as a real person who is principally responsible for the text about himself or herself by the sign of the name on the title page. As to whether the text is sufficiently focused on this person to qualify as an autobiography, that is a matter of critical judgment in each case. Not surprisingly, the Victorian autobiographers who most successfully incorporate a coherent, literary sense of selfhood into their self-history are in fact professional writers. All the autobiographers studied here were published authors, but their identity as writers is significant not only because they have learned a relatively sophisticated method of expressing "selfhood" in language. In the tradition of Edward Gibbon, the typical Victorian literary autobiographer stresses the development of innate traits into mature ideas, but the author's life in effect merges with a chronology of his or her published works as soon as the author has reached the stage of development identified with a public role as he or she wishes to define it. This powerful tendency to make memories of life experience, with its myriad details, conform to works, with their documentary presence and their status in the public sphere (indeed res gestae in a palpable form), creates enormous formal pressures. Assuming that the autobiography will take its ultimate place on the bookshelf at the end of one's collected works, it must serve as a key to interpreting and evaluating the others, if not itself offering a culminating, definitive statement of life philosophy. Newman, Mill, Martineau, Darwin, Spencer, and Galton are especially intent on offering this statement, but to varying degrees, they also express an attachment to their publications as objects and as *commodities*. For all his obsession with abstract ideas, Spencer is almost pathetically sensitive to the failure of his publications—largely underrated and underappreciated in his estimation—to support him comfortably in a capitalist society, while Martineau is equally sensitive to the relative financial success of her own. The novelists Besant and Trollope, especially Trollope, offer the most extreme examples of defining their literary careers in commercial terms, but this strategy is part of a larger one as they position themselves for posthumous public reputations. It is ironic that writers must give up their ideas and creations, must alienate them from themselves through publication before they can be said to own them, for ownership can only be validated in public, social terms through printing and the publication process. In terms of autobiography, this

Conclusion

can be said about the very selfhood the author "creates." As Mill says, the autobiographer must make this move before a less-qualified biographer does instead: "I must be conscious that no one is so well qualified as myself to describe the series of my thoughts and actions" (2).

But, again, the pressures on the writer are formidable, and they are translated into the characteristic tensions of the autobiographical narrative. Before he can enter the final stage of his mental development Mill must go through his mental crisis. When Darwin's life story becomes identical to his bibliography, it does so through the agency of his debilitating "nervous" disease. Spencer goes on and on, but just as surely becomes a machine for writing and publication, retreating from every other form of social activity. Martineau's seemingly miraculous recovery from her first near-fatal illness coincides with a new life philosophy and a rejuvenated will to live and write, but the act of writing for her remains compulsive and alienating, as it is for Darwin and Spencer (public contact with the autobiographical text being deferred until posthumous publication), tied to the concept of duty and the role of prophet. Galton's physical and social environment also is drastically reduced by bodily illness, as he struggles to articulate his one central issue, or cause, of eugenics. Ruskin, as we have seen, refuses to become an adult in his narrative, just as he refuses to specify and defend his true prophetic business in life, as expressed by his many controversial publications. There is one clear implication: if Ruskin confronts his adult, controversial self, he will slip into madness. And yet he is able to locate an essential aspect of himself, his visionary love of natural phenomena, that has remained stable and uncontaminated by the struggle and that he can share with the public. Of course, Darwin, Spencer, Martineau, and Ruskin in their "real" lives probably were neurotic, hypochondriacal people, but that is not my main point. The genre of autobiography as defined here, with its conventional pressures applied through historicity and verifiability, works toward the conflation of personal (interior) development and the (outer) development of career and reputation based on publications (along with other *public* works). Illness is one strategy (and plot function) for controlling the linear development and (vertical) meaning of the narrative. (Let us not forget Newman's metaphor of the deathbed for the crisis that ended the Anglican stage of his self-development.)

Illness is only the most common of the plot functions that provide decisive turning points in the autobiographies and work toward the conflation of inner and outer development. Martineau's initial success with her political economy series, Trollope's arrival in Ireland, the twist of fate that allowed Darwin to sail on the *Beagle*, Gosse's decision to strike out on his own, and (similarly, though not so dramatically) Owen's decision to become an American citizen—each incident has a remarkably decisive impact on the narrative. In each of the final two cases, of course, it provides the life transition that concludes the fragmentary narrative.

The plots of Victorian autobiographies are highly variable in terms of developing motifs and tropes. Autobiographers undergo spiritual and mental crises, live out Romantic and biblical myths, follow historical and scientific paradigms and the dynamic patterns of their own ideas. When we view the autobiographer's plots or "personal myths" at a higher level of abstraction, however, we see that they are composed of relatively simple syntagms (sequences of life events or "functions" that mediate between interior and outer development). When the length of an autobiography approaches the length of a typical Victorian novel, as in the cases of Martineau and Spencer, we find that the autobiographer pauses in the midst of the details to carefully outline a straightforward plot of self-development coordinated with developing theory as expressed in individual publications.

When Victorian autobiographies are studied as representatives of a single genre rather than specialized subgroups, various kinds of intertextuality that result from the larger Victorian culture become more apparent. The parent-son relationships in the works by Mill and Gosse have been the subject of a great deal of analysis, of course, but it is interesting to compare the cases of Mill and Gosse to that of Owen, whose identity is to an even greater extent overshadowed by the historical presence of a famous father. As the personalities of the fathers and sons differ, so do the dynamics of each father-son relationship and the strategies adopted by each author-son to define his independent identity. Nor are parallels limited to the cases of very famous fathers. The father-son relationship is also strongly foregrounded by Spencer, and only slightly less so by Darwin and Galton, and, in spite of the inevitable tensions and conflicts, is described on the whole as a primarily positive and creative force. It might be asked how this compares with the relationship between Martineau and her mother; Martineau apparently relied primarily on male models of writing and scholarship, but her attitude toward her mother is ambivalent and complex. Then there is the fascinating instance of Trollope, in whose narrative the role of the strong Victorian patriarch is reversed and the heroic, novelist mother serves as the son's primary—though not fully acknowledged—role model. Finally, there is Ruskin, dominated by a strong-willed, puritanical mother but also supported both emotionally and financially by a sympathetic and indulgent father. In all these cases, the parent-child relationship can be adequately understood only in the historical context: not only the gender and family role models characteristic of the age, which, among other things, help account for the meek, weak mother figures that Mill virtually ignores and Spencer discounts (with much more sympathy) but also the religious fanaticism of Philip Gosse, the radical politics and prophetic stance of Robert Owen, the bourgeois snobbishness and ambition of the upwardly mobile Ruskins, and so on.

An example of a motif that has less thematic and structural significance and yet illustrates the cultural continuities running through the autobiographies is the acquisition of an appreciation or a taste for natural, landscape beauty. The central importance for Ruskin of his emotional response to landscape has been long recognized, especially since Francis G. Townsend's influential monograph *Ruskin and the Landscape Feeling*.[4] But it is also true that those autobiographers linked with positivistic, scientific traditions—Mill, Martineau, Darwin, Spencer, and Galton—all think that it is worthwhile to record in their autobiographies incidents that mark their development of a genuine appreciation for the beauty of landscape nature. This taste for natural beauty is often classified along with an appreciation for poetry and music, as a valuable aspect of one's emotional life. For example, Darwin laments his loss of the "exquisite delight" he once found in "fine scenery" just after he has confessed that he can no longer enjoy the plays of Shakespeare nor the poetry of Milton, Gray, Byron, Wordsworth, Coleridge, and Shelley (138).

Perhaps most importantly, a complex and intricate web of cross-references and allusions is seen to be woven throughout the autobiographies when they are viewed as a set—references to social, political, literary, and religious issues in terms of each autobiographer's sense of his or her relative position in the intellectual and cultural community of Victorian England. Trollope and Besant maneuver to position themselves (and their posthumous reputations) within a field of literary and ethical forces, as Darwin, Spencer, and Galton do the same within a field of scientific ones, though in a larger sense, all the autobiographers seem to share the same public of informed general readers (with the possible exception of the American Owen). To cite only one obvious example, Spencer's defensive treatment of his own relationship to the ideas of Darwin in one context and Comte and the Saint-Simonians in another, immediately brings to mind Galton's enthusiastic association of his own ideas with those of his distinguished cousin, Mill's account of his own (supposedly limited) debt to the French positivist philosophers, and Martineau's nostalgic description of her communion with Comte's system of ideas as she translated and condensed his *Philosophie Positive* (389–93).

Apart from their appeal to an implied audience of the general public, the autobiographers explicitly or implicitly address specialized audiences. The *ex morte* narrator can openly address individuals (Darwin's children, Trollope's friend Millais). More subtle is the appeal to factions and subgroups within the public, as in Newman's rhetorical strategies. Most of the autobiographers are in some sense speaking for a cause, a party or church, or an ideology.

As we have seen, one recurrent motif in the autobiographies is advice to young, aspiring writers—and here the narrator can afford to be expansive and fatherly or, in the case of Martineau, motherly. Perhaps the most problematic and interesting aspect of implied audience, however, is the appeal to readers in a more or less distant future. Mill and Gosse argue openly that their life stories are interesting because they are representative or characteristic of the age and therefore will be of interest to future generations, but most of the autobiographers seem to assume or at least hope for posthumous fame of one kind or another. In this study I have concentrated on the reading and publishing conventions of the time in which the autobiographies were written. The question of how and why they are read (or not read) today is another matter. Whether or not their lives are "intrinsically interesting," all of the autobiographers discussed here to some extent claim to have created works or expressed ideas whose value is independent of their personal lives.

Biographers of Victorian figures routinely complain about the reticence shown by their subjects in writing their own lives—for example, "The fact is that Darwin was a man incapable of the exuberant self-revelation that good autobiography demands";[5] and "[Martineau's] *Autobiography* . . . is more concerned with the author's development as a writer and a celebrity than it is with the growth of the psyche. It is less a confessional than a memoir and less an analysis than a narrative."[6] However, when one studies the genre of Victorian autobiography on its own terms in its historical setting, one is less likely to impose ahistorical standards such as that of intensive introspection and of confession *for its own sake*. Victorian autobiographers explore their own personalities and analyze their mental development primarily as a means of explaining or defending their engagement in social discourse and public works, and for a professional writer that is usually a matter of explaining or defending one's oeuvre. Rudyard Kipling speaks for many when he writes,

> And for the little, little span
> The dead are borne in mind,
> Seek not to question other than
> The books I leave behind.[7]

The autobiography itself is often the final book left behind, offered as a hermeneutic key to the others.

Notes

Introduction

1. A concise formulation of the "referential aesthetic" can be found in Paul John Eakin, *Touching the World: Reference in Autobiography* (Princeton: Princeton University Press, 1992), 29–53. Eakin cites Elizabeth Bruss as another major critic who, with Lejeune, has been most successful in establishing a poetics of the genre by focusing "precisely on the reader's recognition of a referential intention in such texts and its consequences for their reception" (29). See Bruss, *Autobiographical Acts: The Changing Situation of a Literary Genre* (Baltimore: Johns Hopkins University Press, 1976). Eakin also refers to other critics who have testified to a "felt difference" in their reading experiences between autobiographies and works taken to be "fictions": James M. Cox, *Recovering Literature's Lost Ground: Essays in American Autobiography* (Baton Rouge: Louisiana State University Press, 1989); Francis Russell Hart, "Notes for an Anatomy of Modern Autobiography," *New Literary History* 1 (1970): 485–511; Norman N. Holland, "Prose and Minds: A Psychoanalytical Approach to Non-Fiction," in *The Art of Victorian Prose*, ed. George Levine and William Madden (New York: Oxford University Press, 1968), 314–37; Barrett J. Mandel, "Full of Life Now," in *Autobiography: Essays Theoretical and Critical*, ed. James Olney (Princeton: Princeton University Press, 1980), 49–72; Roy Pascal, *Design and Truth in Autobiography* (Cambridge: Harvard University Press, 1960); and Louis Renza, "The Veto of the Imagination: A Theory of Autobiography," *New Literary History* 9 (1977): 1–26. In the discussion to follow, I adopt for my use a definition of autobiography formulated by Lejeune and point out how my view of the genre engages those of various other critics, including representative poststructuralist (in particular, deconstructionist) critics.
2. This definition is taken from Donald J. Winslow, ed., *Life Writing: A Glossary of Terms in Biography, Autobiography, and Related Forms* (University Press of Hawaii, 1980), 2. The term was first used by a reviewer in the British *Monthly Review* in 1797, and Robert Southey's use of it in 1809 helped give it currency. It gradually displaced related terms such as *apology, confessions,* and, especially, *memoirs.*

3. Pascal, *Design and Truth*, 13.
4. A. O. J. Cockshut, *The Art of Autobiography in Nineteenth- and Twentieth-Century England* (New Haven: Yale University Press, 1984), 2.
5. In a representative example of generic uncertainty, William L. Howarth includes the classifications "as oratory," "as drama," and "as poetry" in his attempt to define the forms of autobiography ("Some Principles of Autobiography," in Olney, *Autobiography*, 85). The most influential critic in this regard has been Olney himself. For Olney, the effect of any attempt to consider the autobiography as a formal or historical matter "would be to separate it from the writer's life and his personality" (*Metaphors of Self* [Princeton: Princeton University Press, 1972], 3). Additional examples of conflating autobiography with other genres (in particular, the novel) will be discussed below.
6. Philippe Lejeune, "The Autobiographical Pact," in *On Autobiography*, ed. Paul John Eakin, trans. Katherine Leary (Minneapolis: University of Minnesota Press, 1989), 4. Lejeune acknowledges the historical specificity of his definition, which "does not claim to cover more than a period of two centuries (since 1770) and deals only with European literature" (4).
7. Lejeune, in later writings, expresses anxiety lest his definition be used in a dogmatic manner, but he continues to defend it as useful and relevant. See "The Autobiographical Pact (bis)" in *On Autobiography*, 120–21.
8. For example, see Suzanne L. Bunkers, "Subjectivity and Self-Reflexivity in the Study of Women's Diaries as Autobiography," *A/B: Auto/Biography Studies* 5 (1990): 114–23.
9. Gosse's biographer Ann Thwaite comments: "[Gosse] thought he was writing while his memory was 'still perfectly vivid,' but we know how unreliable that memory could be" (*Edmund Gosse: A Literary Landscape, 1849–1928* [Chicago: University of Chicago Press, 1984], 435). On the other hand, Heather Henderson stresses Gosse's use of outright "fictional" devices: "His autobiography brings to the fore the literariness of this supposedly nonfiction genre" (*The Victorian Self: Autobiography and Biblical Narrative* [Ithaca: Cornell University Press, 1989], 162). For Henderson, "Gosse takes us to the very edge of fiction, prompting us to cross the boundary and explore first-person novels with a thinly disguised autobiographical origin" (162). However, to recognize varying degrees of fictionality and a sort of progression from autobiography to autobiographical novel is to ignore the conventions expressed in Lejeune's autobiographical pact. See chapter 10 and notes 15 and 19 below.
10. Linda H. Peterson, building on an observation by Wayne Shumaker in *English Autobiography: Its Emergence, Materials, and Form* (Berkeley and Los Angeles: University of California Press, 1954), terms the (Victorian) autobiography a "mixed mode," meaning that in the autobiography, unlike the novel, the hermeneutic mode is characteristically prominent, even dominant over the narrative mode. The narrator often devotes more space to explanation and interpretation than to the actual narration of his story. Unlike Shumaker, who believed that he discerned a welcome evo-

lution of the autobiography to a more fully "novelized" form, Peterson argues, rightly I think, that the "mixed mode" is indigenous and appropriate to the autobiography. See *Victorian Autobiography: The Tradition of Self-Interpretation* (New Haven: Yale University Press, 1986), 4–5.

11. As early as the 1970s, Eugene Vance and Paul de Man were questioning whether autobiography or any other literature can refer to a "self" or "life" prior to the (self-referential) text itself. See especially de Man, "Autobiography as Self-Defacement," *Modern Language Notes* 94 (1979): 919–30. For Michel Foucault the very concept of author represents a repressive "principle of thrift in the proliferation of meaning" in a text and should be abandoned. See "What Is an Author?" in *Textual Strategies*, ed. Josué V. Harari (Ithaca: Cornell University Press, 1979), 153. See also Michael Sprinker, "Fictions of the Self: The End of Autobiography," in Olney, *Autobiography*, 321–42; and Paul Smith, *Discerning the Subject* (Minneapolis: University of Minnesota Press, 1988).

12. See William C. Spengemann, *The Forms of Autobiography* (New Haven: Yale University Press, 1980), 132–65.

13. James Olney, "Some Versions of Memory/Some Versions of Bios: The Ontology of Autobiography," in Olney, *Autobiography*, 248–67.

14. de Man, "Autobiography as Self-Defacement."

15. Lejeune, "The Autobiographical Pact," 13. In extending the argument for referentiality in autobiography, Eakin offers a critique of Roland Barthes's *Roland Barthes by Roland Barthes*, probably the most widely discussed poststructuralist autobiography or antiautobiography, in which Barthes sees himself operating within a wholly self-contained signifying system, so that any question of reference is moot (*Touching the World*, 6). Eakin locates a fundamental ambivalence in Barthes, who insists that the subject of his autobiography is merely linguistic, a product of discourse, and yet desires a discourse of bodies or "pure presence" that is unmediated by speech (8). Drawing on Johnnie Gratton's essay "*Roland Barthes par Roland Barthes:* Autobiography and the Notion of Expression" (*Romance Studies* 8 [1986]: 57–65), Eakin argues that Barthes is "an autobiographer in spite of himself" who finally is unable to read autobiography as fiction (17). Eakin goes on to discuss Barthes's self-professed attempt to "escape from the prison house of critical metalanguage" and "close the gap between private experience and public discourse" in his late works, as reported by J. Gerald Kennedy in "Roland Barthes, Autobiography, and the End of Writing," *Georgia Review* 35 (1981): 381–98. Throughout his study of twentieth-century autobiographies, Eakin insists that autobiography is "nothing if not a referential art," although he concedes that it is also a kind of fiction: "The presumption of truth-value is experientially essential; it is what makes autobiography matter to autobiographers and their readers" (*Touching the World*, 30). I suppose that Eakin's assertion may be considered controversial by some critics of modern autobiography, but the "presumption of truth value" was certainly central to the genre as understood by Victorian autobiographers and their readers.

16. Burton Pike, "Time in Autobiography," *Comparative Literature* 28 (1976): 327. Although I have excluded Wordsworth's autobiographical poem *The Prelude* from consideration here, it is interesting to note that David Ellis in his book *Wordsworth, Freud, and the Spots of Time: Interpretation in "The Prelude"* (Cambridge: Cambridge University Press, 1985) assumes an "autobiographical pact" similar to Lejeune's: "I am reluctant to treat any episode in *The Prelude* exclusively from the point of view of its language or as if . . . there were no distinctions to be drawn between autobiography and fiction" (12). Ellis refers with approval to Sigmund Freud's "instinctive belief that the truth of reality of an individual's past can be a legitimate object of enquiry" in the face of pressures to consider his patients' accounts as no more than fantasies projected back into childhood (11–12). See chapter 6, note 4.
17. Harriet Taylor's contribution to Mill's autobiography will be discussed briefly in chapter 2.
18. I pass over the issue of whether *Sartor Resartus* should be classified as a novel or whether it is sui generis; I am merely arguing that it is misleading to call it an autobiography. The concept of the implied author in autobiography is discussed below. See especially note 32.
19. Jonathan Loesberg discusses this feature in the autobiographies of Mill and Newman at length in *Fictions of Consciousness* (New Brunswick, N.J.: Rutgers University Press, 1986). As his title suggests, Loesberg refers to the author-narrator's position of self-conscious reflection as "fictional." Loesberg admits that it could be claimed that autobiographers select and shape their material without actually falsifying it. "But, if the formulation of self-consciousness with which one shapes one's life has an extra-autobiographical importance as the delineation of a philosophical mediation, the events one relates become valuable as an ostensibly empirical defense of one's theoretical position." The next step for the autobiographer is to "create the empirical evidence that defend[s] the theory. At this point both the controlling order and the events of an autobiography become fictional" (16). However, Loesberg does not treat autobiographies as novels: "Victorian autobiographies are not intended as fictions. . . . If they did not exist *as factual evidence* for mediating positions in the dispute between institutional and experiential theories of knowledge, they would be valueless in that dispute" (13).
20. In his *Confessions*, Augustine, after tracing the history of his old, degenerate self up to the point of his conversion to Christianity and thus his "true," redeemed self in Books 1–9, concludes his temporal narrative. Books 10–13 are composed of historical and theological meditations.
21. See Lejeune, "The Autobiographical Pact," 6–8. Probably the best-known English-language autobiography written in the third person is *The Education of Henry Adams* (1907) by Henry Adams.
22. Lejeune, "The Autobiographical Pact," 11.
23. Ward (whose father was Tom Arnold, brother of Matthew Arnold) discusses her works to some extent but does not focus on a narrative of

self-development. See Mrs. Humphry Ward (Mary Augusta Ward), *A Writer's Recollections* (New York: Harper and Brothers, 1918).

24. A major exception from the Victorian period is the autobiography of J.A. Symonds, which gives a frank account of his homosexuality. See *The Memoirs of John Addington Symonds*, ed. Phyllis Grosskurth (New York: Random House, 1984). Of course Symonds assumed that his autobiography would not be published until long after his death (if it were published at all). Grosskurth terms it "unique in the history of the genre during the nineteenth century" (15). In comparing Symonds's work to more conventional autobiographies, she comments that "[t]o a post-Freudian generation, the autobiographies of Mill, Newman and Ruskin are as interesting for what they fail to say as for what they do tell us" (14). Symonds is also unusual in that "he expresses no passionate involvement or delight in his work" (24). Nevertheless, Symonds's autobiography is conventional in other important ways. He outlines distinct phases in his personal development, speculates about innate personal traits (including homosexual desire), and devotes a chapter to the evolution of his religious opinions. And although he does not argue for his (public) life's work as a critic of literature and art with the enthusiasm characteristic of the other autobiographers (with the exception of Ruskin), he does in fact provide a great deal of bibliographical information about it and ends with a literal catalog of his publications for the preceding twelve years. He does express enthusiasm for those works (published and unpublished) that incorporate his idealized vision of homosexual love and obviously anticipates a future sympathetic audience.

25. This is Peterson's thesis in *Victorian Autobiography*. In addition, Henderson finds the patterns of typological readings of Scripture in Newman's *Apologia*, Ruskin's *Praeterita*, and Gosse's *Father and Son*, and in the three works as a whole a progression from "conversion" to "unconversion" to "subversion." See *The Victorian Self*. Henderson differentiates her work from Peterson's by stressing narrative rather than hermeneutics (11).

26. Shumaker, *English Autobiography*, 27.

27. McKeon derives his concept of "simple abstraction" from Karl Marx's *Grundrisse*. See Michael McKeon, *The Origins of the English Novel, 1600–1740* (Baltimore: Johns Hopkins University Press, 1987), 14–22.

28. Lejeune observes that "[a]utobiography is a literary genre which, by its very content, best marks the confusion of author and person, confusion on which is founded the whole practice and problematic of Western literature since the end of the eighteenth century" ("The Autobiographical Pact," 20).

29. Edward Gibbon, *Memoirs of My Life*, ed. Georges A. Bonnard (New York: Funk and Wagnalls, 1966), 157.

30. In an essay entitled "The Hero as Man of Letters" Carol T. Christ discusses the "man of letters" in terms of the heroic, decidedly *masculine* ideal put forward by Carlyle in his essay on Johnson, Rousseau, and Burns (in *Victorian Sages and Cultural Discourse: Renegotiating Gender and*

Power, ed. Thaïs E. Morgan [New Brunswick, N.J.: Rutgers University Press, 1990], 19–31). For Carlyle, the man of letters is a "specifically modern phenomenon," "someone who sells his writing in a marketplace economy to make a living." However, in following T. W. Heyck's discussion of men of letters in *The Transformation of Intellectual Life in Victorian England* (London: Croom Helm, 1982), Christ points out that men of letters were usually generalists who were not interested in the production of new knowledge, and this is true neither of Gibbon nor Spencer. At any rate, the term is patently gender specific and itself suggests the cultural barrier encountered by Martineau in her deliberate attempt to establish herself as a popular writer of nonfiction prose.

31. The *Memoirs* appeared in 1796, only two years after Gibbon's death, at the beginning of the *Miscellaneous Works of Edward Gibbon, Esq.*, edited by John Holroyd, Earl of Sheffield. The *Memoirs* were printed separately in 1827, and again several times in the course of the nineteenth century. A modern scholarly edition that incorporates portions of Gibbon's manuscripts long unavailable is that of Georges A. Bonnard, cited in note 29. Bonnard discusses the publication history of Gibbon's autobiography in his preface (vii–xxxiii).

32. I use the term *implied author*, introduced by Wayne Booth in *The Rhetoric of Fiction* (Chicago: University of Chicago Press, 1961), because it has acquired a certain currency. However, my concept of the author as an "interpretive construct" from the text that is distinguished from the historical writer is closer to the "postulated author" or "author figure" discussed by Alexander Nehamas in the essay "Writer, Text, Work, Author," in *Literature and the Question of Philosophy*, ed. Anthony J. Cascardi (Baltimore: Johns Hopkins University Press, 1987), 267–91. For Nehamas, this author figure is not correlated only with individual works but is "transcendental in relation to its whole *oeuvre*" (274). Nehamas believes that a transcendental conception of the author is essential for understanding literary interpretation. Of course, both Booth and Nehamas are working exclusively with fiction. Turning to the genre of autobiography as practiced by the Victorians, we see that here, too, each text "generates" an author figure, but the reader assumes that he or she is to interpret the text so that this figure is made consistent with the narrator, the protagonist, and the historically verifiable author of the text, who is supposed to verify the truth of the text. One of the principal tasks of the Victorian autobiographer seems to be guiding the reader in the effort to reconcile the implied authors from previous published texts, whether fictional or nonfictional, to form a consistent interpretive context.

33. See Jack Stillinger, *Multiple Authorship and the Myth of Solitary Genius* (New York: Oxford University Press, 1991), 193.

34. Jerome McGann develops this concept in *A Critique of Modern Textual Criticism* (Chicago: University of Chicago Press, 1983).

35. See chap. 2, note 1.

Notes to Pages 12–24 173

36. See Clinton Machann, "Ruskin's *Praeterita* and Nineteenth-Century Autobiographical Genre," *English Language Notes* 16 (1978): 156–67.
37. A. Dwight Culler claims that "by far the most pervasive paradigm in the nineteenth century is the parallel between the life of the individual and the life-cycle of civilizations." See *The Victorian Mirror of History* (New Haven: Yale University Press, 1985), 280. Karl J. Weintraub argues that "the modern mode of self-conception as an individuality" and "the recognition of a strong historical dimension of all human reality" developed simultaneously in the late eighteenth century and are closely related. See "Autobiography and Historical Consciousness," *Critical Inquiry* 1 (1975): 847.

Chapter 1

1. For a more complete account of the origins of the *Apologia*, see Martin J. Svaglic, "Why Newman Wrote the *Apologia*," in *Newman's "Apologia": A Classic Reconsidered*, ed. V. F. Blehl and F. X. Connolly (New York: Harcourt, Brace & World, 1964), 1–25. It is reprinted in David J. DeLaura's edition of the *Apologia* (New York: W. W. Norton, 1968).
2. Linda H. Peterson, "Newman's *Apologia pro Vita Sua* and the Traditions of the English Spiritual Autobiography," *PMLA* 100 (1985): 300–314.
3. Peterson, "Newman's *Apologia*," 309–10.
4. Throughout this book I use the term *plot functions*, adapted from the Russian structuralist Vladimir Propp, to mean units of action which appear in a narrative in a certain sequence. See *Morphology of the Folktale*, trans. Laurence Scott (Austin: University of Texas Press, 1968).
5. See Martin J. Svaglic, "The Structure of Newman's *Apologia*," *PMLA* 66 (1951): 138–48; and Robert A. Colby, "The Poetical Structure of Newman's *Apologia pro Vita Sua*," *Journal of Religion* 33 (1953): 47–57. Both articles are reprinted in DeLaura's edition of the *Apologia*.
6. See Robert A. Colby, "The Structure of Newman's *Apologia pro Vita Sua* in Relation to His Theory of Assent," *Dublin Review*, no. 460 (1953): 140–56. The article is reprinted in DeLaura's edition of the *Apologia*.
7. Newman is the one autobiographer among our group of Victorians who is included by John Holloway in his classic study of the Victorian "sage" tradition. (Holloway claims that he is showing the view of life mediated through "the whole weave of a book" rather than persuasive techniques as such.) See *The Victorian Sage: Studies in Argument* (London: Macmillan, 1953), 158–201.
8. Walter Houghton, *The Art of Newman's "Apologia"* (New Haven: Yale University Press, 1945), 78.
9. Houghton, *Art*, 78, 80, 82. Referring to Newman's account of his final departure from Oxford, which shows his sense of the dramatic, Houghton writes, "It was equally intended . . . to end his story with the pathetic picture of a kind, affectionate man, heart-sick and lonely, leav-

ing his old home forever. And to this is added very discreetly the image of persecution" (84).
10. See David J. DeLaura, "Newman's *Apologia* as Prophecy," in *Apologia pro Vita Sua*, ed. DeLaura, 492–503.

Chapter 2

1. See especially Jack Stillinger, "Who Wrote J. S. Mill's *Autobiography*?" *Victorian Studies* 27 (1983): 7–23. A revised version of this essay is incorporated into Stillinger's *Multiple Authorship*, 50–68. Referring to Harriet (Taylor) Mill's editing of the first draft, Stillinger reports that "[h]er pencilings appear in 93 of the 169 leaves . . . and affect three hundred passages of text ranging in length from single words to entire pages. In only a very few instances . . . did Mill not approve of or make some change in response to her markings" (*Multiple Authorship*, 51). In addition to Harriet Mill's heavy editing of the first draft, the text was further altered ("corrupted") by Mill's stepdaughter Helen Taylor and others during preparation of the transcript for the first edition, not to mention changes made during printing and the correction of proofs. Stillinger believes that the published text should be at least considered "a collaboration of two authors." However, even though Harriet Mill's intervention in Mill's autobiographical text is profound, her role does not approach that of ghostwriter. In discussing extreme cases of collaboration in autobiography such as that of the ghostwriter, Phillipe Lejeune comments, "[W]hether it is concealed, half-admitted, or openly displayed, collaboration in any case rarely leads the writer to accede to the strategic place reserved for the 'author': the signature. The facts don't matter. It is the logic of the reading contract that is at issue." See "Autobiography of Those Who Do Not Write," in *On Autobiography*, 195.
2. Introduction to John Stuart Mill, *Autobiography and Other Writings*, ed. Jack Stillinger (Boston: Houghton Mifflin, 1969), ix.
3. John M. Morris, *Versions of the Self* (New York: Basic, 1966), 6.
4. Robert Langbaum, *The Poetry of Experience* (New York: Random House, 1957), 20.
5. In revising the early draft of his autobiography, Mill generally toned down his criticism of his father's severity and other personal flaws. As Jack Stillinger puts it, "[T]he later draft comes considerably closer than the earlier to being, in the passages describing him, a eulogy of his father." See the introduction to *The Early Draft of John Stuart Mill's "Autobiography,"* ed. Jack Stillinger (Urbana: University of Illinois Press, 1961), 13.
6. See the introduction to this volume.

Chapter 3

1. Most scholarly commentary on *Threading My Way* is concerned with Owen's account, in the latter sections of the book, of the American social

experiments in which he participated. See, for example, Kathleen Edgerton Kendall and Jeanne Y. Fisher, "Frances Wright on Women's Rights: Eloquence Versus Ethos," *Quarterly Journal of Speech* 60 (1974): 58–68; and Hyman Mariampolski and Dana C. Hughes, "The Use of Personal Documents in Historical Sociology," *American Sociologist* 13 (1978): 104–13.
2. See Richard William Leopold, *Robert Dale Owen: A Biography* (Cambridge: Harvard University Press, 1940), 360–78.
3. Owen was especially unfortunate in that his *Atlantic* article endorsing Katie King appeared after he had already repudiated the "Philadelphia materializations" with which she was associated (Leopold, *Robert Dale Owen*, 402–3). Owen's books on the subject of spiritualism were *Footfalls on the Boundary of Another World* (1860) and *The Debatable Land between This World and the Next* (1870). Although Owen was serious about his own spiritualist beliefs and although he personally investigated rappings, spirit writing, materializations, and other spiritualist phenomena, he was always suspicious of charlatans and "professional believers" connected with the movement and thus was especially sensitive to charges of fraud.
4. See Leopold, *Robert Dale Owen*, 125, 160–61.
5. See Leopold, *Robert Dale Owen*, 144–45, 166–68.
6. See Leopold, *Robert Dale Owen*, 221–34.
7. It is possible that Owen's courtship of Lottie Kellog, which began at about the same time that he began to write his autobiography, contributed to his nostalgic state of mind. His new friend reminded him of his wife, who had died in August 1871. Owen later dedicated *Threading My Way* to Miss Kellog, and they were married in 1876. See Leopold, *Robert Dale Owen*, 412.
8. Paper 12 of Owen's autobiography, "Close of the Tentative Years," apparently was written specially as a conclusion to the book and had not been published in journal form. Owen's final autobiographical articles to appear in the *Atlantic Monthly* included two based on his experiences in Naples and three on his studies of "spiritual phenomena," concluding with "Touching Visitants from a Higher Life," *Atlantic Monthly*, Jan. 1875, 57–69, which dealt with Katie King. (See note 3 above.) Though there is evidence that Owen planned to publish another volume of autobiography, the *Atlantic* articles do not indicate a willingness to treat either his career as a free-thought radical or his career in state and national politics in any depth.
9. Leopold, *Robert Dale Owen*, 308.
10. Leopold, *Robert Dale Owen*, 308. For an account of Robert Owen's belief in spiritualism, see Frank Podmore, *Robert Owen: A Biography* (London: George Allen, 1906), 600–614. Also see Russell M. Goldfarb and Clare R. Goldfarb, *Spiritualism and Nineteenth-Century Letters* (Rutherford, N.J.: Farleigh Dickinson University Press, 1978), 123–24, on both father and son.

Chapter 4

1. *The Autobiography of Harriet Martineau* was published in three volumes by Smith, Elder, and Company in 1877, but the complete text of the autobiography was accommodated by the first two volumes, which Martineau had printed soon after she had written them, in order to ensure their being published in an unaltered state after her death. (Her friends John Chapman, Richard Monckton Milnes, and Henry George Atkinson were allowed to read the manuscript.) The third volume was to consist of memorials written by her friend Maria Weston Chapman at Martineau's request in order to bring the autobiographical account up to date. See Valerie Kossew Pichanick, *Harriet Martineau: The Woman and Her Work, 1802–76* (Ann Arbor: University of Michigan Press, 1980), 202. Chapman was totally sympathetic to her friend but expressed regret that Martineau did not die a Christian and otherwise showed her misunderstanding of Martineau's ideas and attitudes.
2. To be strictly accurate, Martineau reports in her introduction that she began with two earlier autobiographical fragments about her childhood: "Twice in my life I made a beginning; once in 1831, and again about ten years later, during my long illness at Tynemouth: but both attempts stopped short at an early period, answering no other purpose than preserving some facts of my childhood which I might otherwise have forgotten (1)." Martineau understands the importance of the unified, retrospective point of view: "I thought it best to rewrite the early portion, that the whole might be offered from one point of view, and in a consistent spirit" (1–2).
3. Martineau writes this short introduction, which functions as a kind of justification or apologia for her decision to publish her autobiography but not her letters, in the midst of writing about "Period 3" of her life (from age seventeen to age thirty), which includes the major transitions associated with losing her Unitarian faith and achieving her first success as an author.
4. Martineau's commitment to the public discourse characteristic of the "male-dominated" autobiography rather than the private discourse that is now sometimes seen as gender neutral or female dominated is related to her controversial use of the "logocentric" language that some critics connect with the "Victorian sage" tradition. See note 12 below. Of course, Martineau, like most other Victorian autobiographers, quotes from private letters for specific reasons.
5. Harriet Taylor is at least partially responsible for the lack of detail concerning Mill's personal and family life. See chap. 2, note 1.
6. Pichanick describes Martineau as a "devoted disciple" of the Unitarian minister and educator Lant Carpenter at this time in her life (*Harriet Martineau*, 11). It was Carpenter who introduced her to the works of Locke and Hartley.

7. From Marcet, Martineau derived the technique of teaching the principles of political economy by narrative illustration. Like Marcet, Martineau would seek to popularize rather than introduce ideas; unlike Marcet, who wrote primarily for an audience of children, Martineau would aim her works at the adult general public.
8. Martineau is particularly critical of the Whig statesman Lord Brougham, who apparently promised to pay her a sum of money for producing a series of pamphlets on Poor Law reform under the auspices of the Diffusion Society but never fulfilled his promise. See 1:219–21.
9. Martineau sometimes refers to her illness as lasting five years and, at other times, as lasting six.
10. See Pichanick on Martineau's anxieties concerning her mother, Aunt Lee, and, for a time, her brother Henry, all of whom lived with her in a small house on Fludyer Street in London (*Harriet Martineau*, 111–14). However, she argues that Martineau's illness was not inspired by a "hysterical" need for attention or "escapism," as others have suggested (122).
11. The central attraction of mesmerism for Martineau was that it was supposed to rely on physical rather than spiritual properties of the body. Anton Mesmer (1734–1815), founder of the mesmeric school, believed that each individual possesses a "magnetic fluid." By a method involving passes of the hands, a practitioner could "magnetize" the patient and "draw out" his pain. Through Greenhow, who was married to her sister Elizabeth, Martineau was introduced to a visiting mesmerist, Spencer Hall, who initiated Martineau's treatments. Greenhow himself remained skeptical, however, and published an account of Martineau's illness that led to Martineau's alienation from the Greenhows. The continuing controversy over Martineau's *Letters on Mesmerism* led directly to a break with her mother, her brother James, and most of the rest of her family. (Her brother Robert and her sister Ellen remained loyal to her.) Pichanick gives a detailed account of this controversy (129–41). Along with Atkinson, Martineau also came to believe in the scientific basis of phrenology.
12. Curiously, Peterson points out the *myth* that only women gossip and then goes on to treat gossip as a distinctively feminine mode of discourse. She admits that this mode is "a generic feature of some Victorian autobiography: the *res gestae* memoir, as distinct from the developmental autobiography" ("Harriet Martineau: Masculine Discourse, Female Sage," in Morgan, *Victorian Sages*, 171–86). I am arguing that Victorian autobiography can be discussed more meaningfully if the somewhat artificial distinction between res gestae and "real" autobiography is dissolved, and Martineau is a case in point. Since Martineau so obviously treats her writing career at least in part as a substitute for marriage and family life, it might be tempting to look for gender-specific language in the description of her publications; however, male autobiographers typically are just as obsessed with their own works and describe them with equal affection. And it is some of the male autobiographers—not Martineau—who refer to their publications in explicitly sexual imagery. Gib-

bon himself notes the loss of his "litterary [sic] maidenhead" with a youthful essay, recalls "the place and moment of conception" of his *Decline and Fall of the Roman Empire*, and describes the "final deliverance" as he writes the final lines of his great history. See Gibbon, *Memoirs of My Life*, 103, 136, and 180. As we will see below, Spencer compares the "offspring of the mind" to the "offspring of the body" (1:406). When I referred to this metaphor in one of my graduate seminars, a female student assured me that a male author was much more likely than a female author to use such language. But soon after, turning to the preface of Liz Stanley's *The Auto/Biographical I* (Manchester: Manchester University Press, 1992), I read, "This book has had an elephantine gestation period, although its precise moment of fertilization was in December 1982."

13. See Peterson, "Harriet Martineau," 183–86.

Chapter 5

1. R. H. Super, a recent biographer of Trollope, describes the book as "one of the best of all autobiographies" and one that dominates our thinking about Trollope (*The Chronicler of Barsetshire* [Ann Arbor: University of Michigan Press, 1988], vii).
2. See Super, *The Chronicler of Barsetshire*, 351; and N. John Hall, *Trollope: A Biography* (Oxford: Clarendon Press, 1991), 411–12. Contemporary reviews of Trollope's autobiography were generally favorable.
3. Super suggests that Trollope probably read Mill's *Autobiography* shortly after it was published in 1873 and points to the similarity between Trollope's modest disclaimer of his own significance at the beginning of the book and a similar opening statement by Mill (*The Chronicler of Barsetshire*, 350).
4. Super speculates that in writing about his own rather miserable youth Trollope may have been influenced by Charles Dickens's autobiographical fragment describing his miserable childhood experiences in the infamous Warren's Blacking warehouse (*The Chronicler of Barsetshire*, 351).
5. For example, Howard Helsinger believes that "Trollope's difficulty in establishing a basis for credibility stems from his ambivalent desire to be both common and unique." See "Credence and Credibility: The Concern for Honesty in Victorian Autobiography," in *Approaches to Victorian Autobiography*, ed. George P. Landow (Athens: Ohio University Press, 1979), 48.
6. The most comprehensive treatment of Trollope's ideal of the gentleman is Shirley Robin Letwin, *The Gentleman in Trollope: Individuality and Moral Conduct* (Cambridge: Harvard University Press, 1982).

Chapter 6

1. On the writing of *Praeterita* see Wolfgang Kemp, *The Desire of My Eyes: The Life and Work of John Ruskin*, trans. Jan van Heurck (New York: Farrar, Straus and Giroux, 1990), 427–56.

2. See, for example, Claudette Kemper Columbus, "Ruskin's *Praeterita* as Thanatography," in Landow, *Approaches to Victorian Autobiography*, 109–27.
3. See especially Van Akin Burd, "Another Light on the Writing of *Modern Painters*," *PMLA* 68 (1953): 755–63, and "Ruskin's Quest for a Theory of the Imagination," *Modern Language Quarterly* 17 (1956): 60–72. In describing Ruskin's childhood Tim Hilton observes, "Certainly Ruskin's claim in his autobiography that he lacked toys is inaccurate (*John Ruskin: The Early Years* [New Haven: Yale University Press, 1985], 13).
4. In a recent study of Wordsworth's "spots of time" from a psychological point of view, David Ellis confronts the thorny question of their relation to historical or biographical reality. Although it can be shown that Wordsworth occasionally distorted the truth in *The Prelude*, "the impression he nevertheless gives in it is of a man striving to record with precision" (*Wordsworth*, 10). Ellis's remarks here and elsewhere in his study might be applied to Ruskin's *Praeterita* as well. See the introduction, note 16.
5. Ruskin seems to anticipate the language of Roland Barthes in his "anti-autobiography" (see the introduction, note 15). Barthes writes, "Perhaps in places, certain fragments seem to follow one another by some affinity; but the important thing is that these little networks not be connected, that they not slide into a single enormous network which would be the structure of the book, its meaning" (*Roland Barthes by Roland Barthes*, trans. Richard Howard [New York: Farrar, 1977], 148). Since Barthes evidently intends that his autobiography not imply a coherent narrative of development, it is not surprising that his work, like *Praeterita*, is dominated by images of childhood.
6. *Works*, Library Edition, ed. E. T. Cook and Alexander Wedderburn (London: George Allen, 1904), 5:4.
7. Kemp counts a total of twenty-six times (with "variations and abbreviations") that Ruskin actually made this journey along the "old road" (*Desire of My Eyes*, 432).

Chapter 7

1. Ostensibly Darwin wrote his autobiography for the benefit of his immediate family and did not intend that it should be published, but the text displays his "habitual diffidence" nevertheless. See Peter Brent, *Charles Darwin* (New York: Harper and Row, 1981), 494.
2. Darwin's notorious ill health has been studied extensively. See Ralph Colp, Jr., *To Be an Invalid: The Illness of Charles Darwin* (Chicago: University of Chicago Press, 1977). Colp incorporates all the available evidence from Darwin's papers and related historical archives and evaluates previous literature on the subject. He concludes that psychological stresses were the most probable cause for Darwin's symptoms, although Darwin may have suffered from medical illnesses as well (142–43).

Chapter 8

1. Portsmouth was also the birthplace of Charles Dickens, who wrote sketches describing the south coast in his journals *All the Year Round* and *Household Words*. Curiously enough, Besant, who saw himself in some ways as Dickens's successor, died on 9 June 1901. Dickens had died on 9 June 1870.
2. Apparently Besant himself did most of the actual writing, while Rice was chiefly responsible for plot construction and handled all business arrangements with publishers. Records suggest that Besant and Rice were consistently underpaid for their rights to their works. Besant was generally unwilling to involve himself in negotiations with publishers, even after Rice's death: this is ironic in light of Besant's championing of authors' rights and his belief that writers should conduct themselves and be treated like businessmen. See two articles by Simon Eliot, "'His Generation Read His Stories': Walter Besant, Chatto and Windus, and *All Sorts and Conditions of Men*," *Publishing History* 21 (1987): 25–67, and "Unequal Partnerships: Besant, Rice and Chatto 1876–82," *Publishing History* 26 (1989): 73–109.
3. In *All Sorts and Conditions of Men* (1882), which was said by a contemporary reviewer to have "shocked and aroused the conscience of all England" by its portrayal of the dismal conditions in the East End, Besant described the planning and construction of a "Palace of Delight" for the poor. Remarkably, through a public conscription organized by Sir Edmund Currie, a "palace" serving as a "centre of organized recreation, orderly amusement, and intellectual culture," much like that described in Besant's novel, was actually built, and for a time was very successful. Besant's status as a reformer and philanthropist was a major reason for his being knighted in 1895.
4. Besant's aversion for Calvinism and what he called Christian "religiosity" is in evidence in some of his fiction, notably the novella *In Deacon's Orders* (1895). The principal character of that story is a man who, from childhood, relies on an angelic demeanor and an ability to speak in an apparently sincere, emotional manner to lie and cheat his way through life.

Chapter 9

1. The *Autobiography* covers sixty-two years of Spencer's life. Spencer, who lived for an additional twenty-one years after completing the text, intended that the authorized biography of his life by David Duncan, a former secretary who had assisted him in compiling the research for his *Principles of Sociology* (2:201, 252–53), should give the "authoritative record" of the remainder of his life. See *Life and Letters of Herbert Spencer* (New York: D. Appleton, 1908), 1:viii. Spencer even provided Duncan with an "intellectual history" of himself, written in 1898–99, entitled

"The Filiation of Ideas." This long essay, published as an appendix to *Life and Letters* (2:304–65), is an extenuation and an elaboration of the pattern of his intellectual development as described in the *Autobiography*.
2. J. D. Y. Peel notes that "of all the great Victorian sages, Spencer lost his repute soonest" (*Herbert Spencer: The Evolution of a Sociologist* [New York: Basic Books, 1971], 1.) Spencer's careful defense of his reputation in his autobiography apparently did little to impede this "drop into obscurity." Peel explains this rapid decline in two ways: first, "Posterity is cruellest to those [like Spencer] who sum up for their contemporaries in an all-embracing synthesis the accumulated knowledge of their age"; second, unlike Mill, Darwin, and other figures, Spencer was "an institutional outsider, attached to no parties, institutes or universities which might continue his work." Most recent studies of Spencer, like Peel's, emphasize his enormous popular influence, which reached its peak in the 1880s, and the widespread underestimation and occasional misrepresentation of his ideas since the turn of the century. Jonathan H. Turner, in *Herbert Spencer: A Renewed Appreciation* (Beverly Hills, Calif.: Sage Publications, 1985), offers an especially energetic vindication of Spencer's social theory. There is no substantial modern biography of Spencer.
3. The friendship between Spencer and George Eliot, which began in 1851 and continued until her death in 1880, is well known. There is evidence that in the early stages of the relationship Eliot was deeply attracted to him. See Peel, *Herbert Spencer*, 13. One of the few modern treatments of Spencer from a literary point of view is Nancy L. Paxton, *George Eliot and Herbert Spencer: Feminism, Evolutionism, and the Reconstruction of Gender* (Princeton: Princeton University Press, 1991). Paxton believes that an "anxiety of influence" existed between the two as Spencer moved from a feminist to an antifeminist stance in his writings. Given Spencer's characteristic reluctance to recognize intellectual influences (see note 6 below), it is not surprising that his several references to Eliot in his *Autobiography* are not especially revealing on this score.
4. Spencer builds on this scheme in detailing his intellectual history (and thus a "sketch plan" for his entire *Synthetic Philosophy*) in "The Filiation of Ideas," which Duncan describes as his "final contribution to the theory of evolution" (Spencer, *Life and Letters*, ix). See note 1.
5. See for example the references to Spencer's autobiography in the introduction to Landow, *Approaches to Victorian Autobiography*, xxx–xxxiv.
6. On Spencer's disavowal of Comte's influence, see S. Eisen, "Herbert Spencer and the Spectre of Comte," *Journal of British Studies* 7 (1967): 48–67.
7. Duncan includes the text of the short note of 25 November 1858 (1:113), which also had been included in the *Life and Letters of Charles Darwin*, ed. Francis Darwin (London: John Murray, 1887), 1:497. Darwin terms Spencer's development theory "admirable" and says that he might have quoted Spencer's argument "with great advantage," but even here his remark that "I treat the subject as a naturalist, and not from a general

point of view" anticipates his sharp criticism of Spencer, referred to in chapter 7.
8. See Spencer's own "Obituary Notice of J. S. Mill," appendix G of his *Autobiography*, 594–97.

Chapter 10

1. Gosse was known as a rapid writer, but his composition of *Father and Son* was slow and full of anguish. He began to write it in Florence during the fall of 1905. He delivered the manuscript to William Heinemann in May 1907 but at the request of his publisher added the epilogue before the book was published in October of the same year. (Gosse's friend George Moore had suggested that he write the book some fifteen years earlier.) See Ann Thwaite's account of the composition process and the early, very favorable, reception of the book in *Edmund Gosse*, 430–49.
2. On the genre of *Father and Son*, see James D. Woolf, *Sir Edmund Gosse* (New York: Twayne, 1972), 117; Edgar Johnson, "A Dying Puritanism," in *A Treasury of Biography* (New York: Howell, Suskin, 1941), 425; Sir Evan Charteris, *The Life and Letters of Sir Edmund Gosse* (New York: Haskell House, 1973), 302; William J. Gracie Jr., "Truth of Form in Edmund Gosse's *Father and Son*," *Journal of Narrative Technique* 4 (1974):176–85.
3. Thwaite acknowledges that Gosse did at points "rearrange truth," but "probably unwittingly." Gosse did admit privately to Harold Nicolson that "the end had been slightly arranged." Thwaite points out that "there was no total break with his father at twenty-one, as the epilogue suggests." See Thwaite, *Edmund Gosse*, 435.
4. *Omphalos* represented Philip Gosse's attempt to reconcile scientific with biblical discourse. In the words of his son, the thesis was that "there had been no gradual modification of the surface of the earth, or slow development of organic forms, but that when the catastrophic act of creation took place, the world presented, instantly, the structural appearance of a planet on which life had long existed" (86–87). The book was supposed to "bring all the turmoil of scientific speculation to a close, fling geology into the arms of Scripture, and make the lion eat grass with the lamb" (87).
5. See note 1. George Moore in fact advised Gosse to write additional chapters, to bring the story up to the time "when you have got into the British museum and are beginning to make your own living" (quoted in Thwaite, *Edmund Gosse*, 432).
6. Cynthia Northcutt Malone, "The Struggle of *Father and Son*: Edmund Gosse's Polemical Autobiography," *A/B: Auto/Biography Studies* 8 (1993): 16–32. Malone, using the methods of Bakhtinian dialogism, analyzes the "hidden polemic" between Gosse and his father. Other father-son autobiographies, like those of Mill and Owen, would be amenable to this kind of analysis.

7. Malone, "Struggle," 30. Malone points out that in the epilogue Gosse quotes at length from a letter addressed to him by his father, a letter in which he describes his son's development not as progress but as sinful backsliding. She suggests that the letter both frames and opposes the son's account of his progress, turning the epilogue into an epigraph that leads the reader back to the beginning of the narrative and joins the voices of father and son "in a polemical dialogue which always circles back to its beginnings."

Chapter 11

1. Galton wrote his autobiography with remarkable speed. In November 1907 he agreed to his publisher Metheun's proposal that he write it; by the following August he was reading proofs, and *Memories of My Life* was published in October 1908. See D. W. Forrest, *The Life and Work of a Victorian Genius* (London: Paul Elek, 1974), 273–74. No doubt Galton's haste helps to explain some of the organizational problems referred to below.
2. Galton mentions the work of Gregor Mendel with respect (308) but does not realize how soon and how fully Mendel's theory of heredity will render his own obsolete.
3. Forrest notes Galton's reluctance to include the names of women, even prominent women whom he knew, and ties this to an apparent prejudice against women (*Life and Work*, 274).
4. It is possible that Galton's growing obsession with eugenics was in some way connected with his own failure to produce offspring. If so, there is a profound irony in his theories about the superiority of families like his own. According to Forrest, Galton's "growing interest in heredity dates from about the time when it was evident that his marriage [to Louisa Butler] was likely to prove infertile. There is no reason to suppose that the marriage was not consummated. It is more likely that the infertility was genetic: neither of his brothers had children and none of Louisa's sisters" (85).

Conclusion

1. See William Matthews, *British Autobiographies: An Annotated Bibliography of British Autobiographies Published or Written before 1951* (Berkeley and Los Angeles: University of California Press), 1955.
2. Matthews writes that he included a title "only if [the] writer seemed to be mostly concerned with himself" rather than with other matters, but he "claim[s] no consistency in the application of this principle" (*British Autobiographies*, xi).
3. Jerome H. Buckley, *Autobiography and the Subjective Impulse since 1800* (Cambridge: Harvard University Press, 1984), 19. Buckley draws his figures from Richard D. Altick, *Lives and Letters* (New York: Alfred A.

Knopf, 1965), 104. Buckley, however, is primarily interested in what I would call autobiographicality rather than the formal genre of autobiography. Earlier, Keith Rinehart had analyzed the rising interest in autobiographies as the nineteenth century progressed and noted the enormous increase in their publication during the Victorian era. See "The Victorian Approach to Autobiography," *Modern Philology* 51 (1954): 177–86.
4. Francis G. Townsend, *Ruskin and the Landscape Feeling* (Urbana: University of Illinois Press, 1951). In a wider context, Carol T. Christ analyzes the transformations in seeing and analyzing landscape nature that took place in nineteenth-century England in *The Finer Optic* (New Haven: Yale University Press, 1975).
5. Brent, *Charles Darwin*, 494.
6. Pichanick, *Harriet Martineau*, 201–2.
7. Rudyard Kipling, "The Appeal," in *Complete Verse: Definitive Edition* (New York: Doubleday, 1940), 836.

Index

Adams, Henry, 170
Aesop's Fables, 34
Africa, 126, 145, 148, 149, 150, 154, 156
Aikin, John, 55
Ali, Mehemet, 148
Alps, 82, 91
Altick, Richard D., 183
Arian heresy, 18
Arkwright, Richard, 40, 45
Arnold, Matthew, 24, 130, 170; "The Grande Chartreuse," 143
Arnold, Tom, 170
Atheneum, 61
Atheneum Club, 149
Atkinson, Henry G., 61, 62, 63, 176, 177
Atlantic Monthly, 38
Atlantic Union, 112
Augustine, Saint: *Confessions*, 14, 15, 20, 22, 25, 170
Austen, Jane, 54
Autobiography, Victorian: Augustinian coda in, 8, 31, 64, 108, 112, 126, 152; definitions of, 2–12, 159; *ex morte*, 4, 51, 69, 77, 95, 128, 159, 164; as genre, 1–12, 159–65; life-and-career, 10, 12, 27, 51, 69, 74, 88, 96, 102, 107, 113, 118, 124, 128, 133, 135, 140, 146; and memoirs, 2, 3, 9, 37, 58, 66–67, 70, 98, 108, 147, 165; narrative structure of, 3–12, 13–157 passim, 161, 162; and the novel, 2, 6, 7, 8, 10, 11, 12, 69, 70, 72, 73, 75, 76, 79, 107, 108, 111, 115, 136, 140, 159, 160; as a referential art, 1, 6, 167, 169; res gestae, 2, 10, 12, 27, 105, 160; rhetoric in, 2, 15, 22, 24, 36, 37, 45, 66, 76, 77, 86, 92, 93, 94, 102, 114, 128, 142, 153, 164; spiritual, 10, 12, 14–16, 20, 24, 71, 159, 162

Baer, Karl Ernst von, 122, 124
Barlow, Nora, 95
Barthes, Roland, 169, 179
Battle of Waterloo, 54
Beagle, The, 96–97, 99, 101, 103, 104, 105, 113, 126, 162
Bentham, Jeremy, 29, 30, 31, 35
Bentham, Sir Samuel, 28
Bertillon, Alphonse, 154
Besant, Sarah (Besant's mother), 109
Besant, Walter: *All Sorts and Conditions of Men*, 112, 180; *Autobiography*, 1, 107–16, 150, 160, 164, 180; *By Celia's Arbor*, 108; *Children of Gibeon*, 112; *Dorothy Foster*, 111; *The French Humourists*, 111; *In Deacon's Orders*, 180; *Ready Money Mortiboy*, 111; *The Revolt of Man*, 115; "The Survey of London," 112, 115; "Titania's Farewell," 111
Besant, William (Besant's father), 109
Bey, Arnaud, 148
Birmingham Oratory, 25
Birmingham General Hospital, 146
Blackwoods, 83
Blehl, V. F., 173
Bonnard, Georges A., 12, 171, 172
Book of Revelation, 139
Booth, Wayne, 172

Brent, Peter, 179, 184
British Association for the Advancement of Science, 150–51
Brontë, Charlotte, 62
Brougham, Lord (Henry Peter), 57, 177
Bruss, Elizabeth, 167
Buckland, William, 103
Buckley, Jerome H., 159, 183, 184
Bull, Bishop, 16
Bunkers, Suzanne L., 168
Bunyan, John: *Grace Abounding to the Chief of Sinners*, 10, 14
Burd, Van Akin, 179
Burton, Richard, 150
Butler, Bishop Joseph, 16
Byron, George Gordon, Lord, 82, 163

Calvinism, 112–13, 180. *See also* Puritanism
Cambridge University, 96, 97, 103, 105, 109, 112, 146, 147, 152, 153, 154
Carlyle, Thomas, 24, 103, 115, 150, 171, 172; "Characteristics," 33; *Sartor Resartus*, 6, 7, 20, 33, 120, 170
Carpenter, Lant, Reverend, 55, 176
Cascardi, Anthony J., 172
Chapman, Edward, 75
Chapman, John, 176
Chapman, Maria Weston, 65, 176
Charteris, Sir Evan, 182
Christ, Carol T., 171, 172, 184
Clay, Henry, 58
Clough, Arthur Hugh, 139
Cockshut, A. O. J., 3, 167
Colby, Robert A., 20, 173
Coleridge, Samuel Taylor, 31, 35, 163; "Dejection: An Ode," 33
Collins, Wilkie, 7
Colp, Ralph, Jr., 179
Columbus, Claudette Kemper, 179
Comte, Auguste, 30, 31, 32, 62, 64, 66, 122, 129, 164, 181; *Positive Philosophy*, 62, 164

Connolly, F. X., 173
Cook, E. T., 179
Cornhill Magazine, 73
Cox, James M., 167
Culler, A. Dwight, 173
Currie, Sir Edmund, 180

Daily News, 51, 64
Dale, David, 40
Darwin, Charles, 129, 138, 145, 153, 154, 156, 181; *Autobiography*, 1, 11, 12, 64, 67, 77, 95–105, 110, 113, 126, 128, 129, 130, 132, 145, 149, 152, 160, 161, 162, 163, 164, 165, 179; *Cirripedia*, 99; *Effects of Cross- and Self-Fertilization in the Vegetable Kingdom*, 100; *The Formation of Vegetable Mould through the Action of Worms*, 100; *Journal of The Beagle*, 97, 98, 99, 104, 149; *Origin of Species*, 98, 99, 102, 128, 129, 152
Darwin, Emma (Darwin's wife), 98, 102
Darwin, Erasmus (Darwin's grandfather), 145, 157
Darwin, Francis (Darwin's son), 181
Darwin, Robert Waring (Darwin's father), 96, 97, 162
DeLaura, David, 173, 174
Devonshire, 138, 141
Dickens, Charles, 7, 45, 76, 114, 178, 180; *David Copperfield*, 6, 70; *Great Expectations*, 43; *Pickwick Papers*, 139
Dictionary of National Biography, 153, 154
Domecq, Adèle, 83
Domecq family, 88
Dumont, Pierre Etienne Louis, 32
Duncan, David, 180, 181

Eakin, Paul John, 1, 167, 168, 169
East India Company, 28, 29, 72, 78
Economist, 121, 122
Eisen, S., 181
Eliot, Simon, 180

Index

Ellis, David, 170, 179
Emerson, Ralph Waldo, 58, 62
Eugenics, 145, 151, 152, 153, 154, 155, 156, 161
Evans, Mary Ann (George Eliot), 117, 122, 129, 132, 181

Fellenberg, Emmanuel von, 41
Fielding, Henry, 114
Fisher, Jeanne Y., 174
Fitz-Roy, Robert, 97
Ford, Ford Maddox: *Parade's End*, 79
Forrest, D. W., 183
Foucault, Michel, 169
Fox, Charles, 57
Fox, William James, 56, 57
Free Enquirer, 38
Freeling, Sir Francis, 77
Freud, Sigmund, 170
Froude, Hurrell, 16
Froude, James Anthony, 121; *History of England*, 13
Fuller, Margaret, 58, 62

Galton, Francis, 96; *The Art of Travel*, 150; *English Men of Science*, 152; *Hereditary Genius*, 152; "Hereditary Talent and Character," 152; *Human Faculty*, 152; *Memories of My Life*, 1, 145–57, 160, 161, 162, 163, 164, 183; *Natural Inheritance*, 152
Galton, Louisa (Galton's wife), 149, 183
Galton, Samuel Tertius (Galton's father), 146, 147, 148, 156, 162
Garrison, William Lloyd, 58
Geological Society, 100
Gibbon, Edward: *Memoirs of My Life*, 10, 11, 12, 27, 51, 74, 105, 118, 127, 160, 171, 172, 177–78
Globe, 53
Goldfarb, Clare R., 175
Goldfarb, Russell M., 175
Gosse, Edmund: *Father and Son*, 1, 2, 4, 9, 37, 40, 45, 46, 48, 113, 135–43, 162, 163, 164, 168, 171, 182, 183

Gosse, Emily (Gosse's mother), 137, 138
Gosse, Philip Henry (Gosse's father), 135–43 passim, 162, 163, 182; *Omphalos*, 136, 182, 183
Gracie, William J., Jr., 182
Gratton, Johnnie, 169
Gray, Thomas, 163
Greenhow, Elizabeth (Martineau), 177
Greenhow, Thomas, 59, 177
Grosskurth, Phyllis, 171
Grove, Sir William, 151

Hall, N. John, 178
Hall, Spencer, 177
Harari, Josué V., 169
Harrow, 78
Hart, Francis Russell, 167
Hartley, David, 55
Hawkins, Edward, 16, 24
Hawthorne, Nathaniel: *Scarlet Letter*, 6
Helsinger, Howard, 178
Henderson, Heather, 168, 171
Henslow, John Stevens, 97
Heurck, Jan van, 178
Heyck, T. W., 172
Hill, Rowland, 42, 76
Hilton, Tim, 179
Hofwyl (Switzerland), 41
Holland, Norman N., 167
Holloway, John, 173
Holroyd, John (Earl of Sheffield), 11, 172
Homer, 20
Hooker, Joseph D., 98, 99, 103
Hopkins, Gerard Manley: *Journal*, 3
Houghton, Walter, 24, 173
Houlston (publishing house), 56
Howard, Richard, 179
Howarth, William L., 168
Howells, William Dean, 38
Hughes, Dana C., 175
Hume, David: *Life*, 10
Huxley, T. H., 98, 103, 117, 122, 132

Ibsen, Henrik, 135
Immaculate Conception, 21
International Exposition of 1884, 151

Jackson, Andrew, 58
Jerusalem bishopric, 19
"Jessie," 42, 44
Johnson, Edgar, 182

Kant, Immanuel: *The Critique of Pure Reason*, 121
Keats, John: *Endymion*, 139
Kellog, Lottie, 175
Kemp, Wolfgang, 178, 179
Kendall, Kathleen Edgerton, 175
Kennedy, J. Gerald, 169
Kentish, Aunt, 54
Kew Observatory, 151
King, Katie, 39, 175
King Edward's "Free School" (Birmingham), 146
King's College, 109, 146
Kingsley, Charles, 13–14, 24
Kipling, Rudyard, 165, 184
Knowles, Sheridan, 139

La Touche, Rose, 84
Lafayette, General, 42
Lamarck, J. B. de, 131
Landon, Letitia Elizabeth, 42
Landow, George P., 178, 179, 181
Langbaum, Robert, 33, 174
Lavater, Johann Kaspar, 97
Leamington, 109, 112, 149
Leary, Katherine, 168
Lejeune, Phillipe, 1, 3–9, 11, 12, 159, 167, 168, 169, 170, 171, 174
Leopold, Richard William, 175
Letwin, Shirley Robin, 178
Levine, George, 167
Lewes, George H., 117, 121, 122, 132
Livingstone, David, 150, 154
Locke, John, 55
Loesberg, Jonathan, 170
Lott, Edward, 127, 132
Lyle, Sir Charles, 99, 103

Maberly, Colonel, 75
Machann, Clinton, 173
Macmillan's Magazine, 152
Madden, William, 167
Malone, Cynthia Northcutt, 141, 182, 183
Malthus, Thomas: *An Essay on the Principle of Population*, 99
Man of letters, 11, 171–72
Man, Paul de, 169
Mandel, Barrett J., 167
Marcet, Jane: *Conversations on Political Economy*, 56, 177
Mariampolski, Hyman, 175
Marmontel, Jean-François: *Memoirs*, 30
Marshall, John, 58
Martineau, Elizabeth (Martineau's mother), 52, 54, 60, 163, 177
Martineau, Ellen (Martineau's sister), 53
Martineau, Harriet, 172; *Autobiography*, 1, 8, 9, 11, 39, 51–67, 72, 76, 79, 90, 93, 100, 105, 108, 113, 115, 118, 130, 160, 161, 162, 163, 164, 165, 176, 177, 178; *Deerbrook*, 59; *Eastern Life*, 55, 62; "Female Writers on Practical Divinity," 55; *Letters on the Laws of Man's Nature and Development*, 63; *Letters on Mesmerism*, 61; *Life in the Sick-Room*, 60, 64; "Literary Lionism," 58; *The Man and the Hour*, 60; "Political Economy Series," 56, 57; *Retrospect of Western Travels*, 59; *Society in America*, 58, 59, 64
Martineau, Henry (Martineau's brother), 177
Martineau, James (Martineau's brother), 55, 61, 63, 177
Martineau, Thomas (Martineau's father), 52
Matthews, William, 159, 183
Maurice, F. D., 92, 112
Mauritius, 110, 114
McGann, Jerome, 12, 172

Index

McKeon, Michael, 10, 171
Mendel, Gregor, 183
Mesmer, Anton, 177
Mesmerism, 60, 61, 64
Meyers, Walter, Reverend, 16
Middle East, 62
Mill, Harriet (Mill's mother), 163
Mill, Harriet (Taylor) (Mill's wife), 7, 27, 28, 30, 31, 32, 33, 35, 36, 43, 170, 174, 176
Mill, James (Mill's father), 27, 28, 35, 36, 37, 78, 162
Mill, John Stuart, 181, 182; *Autobiography*, 1, 4, 7, 8, 11, 12, 20, 27–36, 37, 42, 48, 51, 52, 54, 63, 64, 65, 72, 79, 89, 90, 93, 101, 105, 110, 115, 119, 121, 126, 128, 129, 130, 131, 136, 141, 147, 160, 161, 162, 163, 164, 170, 171, 174, 176, 178, 182; *Logic*, 31, 120
Millais, John Everett, 77, 164
Milnes, Joseph, 16
Milnes, Richard Monckton, 176
Milton, John, 54, 163; *Paradise Lost*, 53
Monophysites (Eutychians), 18
Monthly Repository, 53, 54, 55, 56
Moore, George, 182
Morgan, Thaïs E., 172
Morris, John N., 33, 174
Multiple authorship, 11, 174
Munchausen, Baron von, 41

Naples, 38, 47
Near East, 145, 147, 148
Necessarianism, 55, 79
Nehamas, Alexander, 172
Nelson, Horatio, Admiral, 53
New Harmony (Indiana), 38, 39, 42, 43, 46, 47
New Lanark, 40, 42, 43, 45
Newman, Francis W., 121
Newman, John Henry: *Apologia pro Vita Sua*, 1, 2, 8, 9, 10, 12, 13–25, 26, 27, 28, 31, 32, 35, 36, 37, 40, 48, 64, 72, 79, 93, 99, 100, 101, 103, 105, 127, 135, 136, 141, 160, 161, 164, 170, 171, 173; *The Church of the Fathers*, 17; *Essay on the Development of Christian Doctrine*, 19, 21; *Grammar of Assent*, 20; *Prophetical Office of the Church*, 17; *Tract*, 18, 90
Newton, Thomas, 16
Nicholas, Grand Duke of Russia, 41
Nicolson, Harold, 182
Nonconformist, 120
Norton, Charles, 84, 85

Oldfield, Edmund, 87
Olney, James, 167, 168, 169
Once a Week, 111
Owen, Ann Caroline Dale (Owen's mother), 48
Owen, Richard, 103
Owen, Robert (Owen's father), 37, 38, 39, 40, 41, 43, 45, 46, 47, 58, 78, 162, 163, 175
Owen, Robert Dale: *The Debatable Land between This World and the Next*, 175; *Footfalls on the Boundary of Another World*, 175; *Moral Physiology*, 38, 39; *Threading My Way: An Autobiography*, 1, 37–49, 52, 64, 65, 75, 78, 162, 163, 164, 174, 175, 182
Oxford Movement, 16, 17, 19, 24
Oxford University, 16, 17, 19, 22, 23, 24, 83, 103

Parkyns, Mansfield, 148
Partridge, Richard, 146
Pascal, Roy: *Design and Truth in Autobiography*, 2, 9, 168
Paxton, Nancy L., 181
Pearson, Karl, 153
Peel, J. D. Y., 181
People's Palace, 112
Perry, Isaac, Reverend, 53
Peterson, Linda H., 5, 14, 66, 168, 169, 171, 173, 177, 178
Pichanick, Valerie Kossew, 176, 177, 184

Pike, Burton, 6, 170
Pilot, 121
Podmore, Frank, 175
Portsmouth, 108
Post office, 70, 71, 72, 73, 75, 76, 77, 78
Poststructuralism, 167, 169
Prichard, William, 121
Priestley, Joseph, 55
Propp, Vladimir, 173
Punch, 155
Puritanism, 136, 137, 139, 141, 143. *See also* Calvinism
Pusey, Edward B., 17

Reade, Charles, 114
Reconstruction (in the United States), 38
Renza, Louis, 167
Rice, James, 107, 111, 180
Rinehart, Keith, 184
Rogers, Samuel: *Italy,* 82
Rousseau, Jean-Jacques, 22, 70
Royal Geographical Society, 149, 150
Royal Society, 149, 153
Ruskin, John, 24, 35, 184; *Fors Clavigera,* 4, 82; *Modern Painters,* 83; "The Poetry of Architecture," 83; *Praeterita,* 1, 2, 4, 12, 24, 37, 39, 45, 81–94, 96, 101, 108, 114, 127, 130, 135, 147, 161, 163, 171, 178, 179; *The Stones of Venice,* 88; "The Storm-Cloud of the Nineteenth Century," 92
Ruskin, John James (Ruskin's father), 82, 87, 88, 89, 163
Ruskin, Margaret (Ruskin's mother), 82, 87, 163

Sabine, Sir Edward, R. A., 153
St. George's Hospital, 146
St. John, Ambrose, 25
Saint-Simonians, 30, 32, 33, 148, 164
Saunders and Otley (publishing house), 59
Scott, Laurence, 173

Scott, Thomas: *The Force of Truth,* 14, 16, 20
Scott, Sir Walter, 114
Severn, Joan, 84
Severn, Joseph, 84, 85
Shakespeare, William, 54, 139; *Midsummer Night's Dream,* 139
Shelley, Mary, 42, 43
Shelley, Percy Bysshe, 35, 163
Shetland Islands, 149
Shumaker, Wayne, 10, 168, 171
Smith, Paul, 169
Smithsonian Institution, 37, 39
Smollett, Tobias George, 114
Society for the Systematic and Scientific Exploration of Palestine, 110, 111
Society of Authors, 112, 115
Southey, Robert, 167
Speke, J. H., 150
Spencer, Harriet (Spencer's mother), 131
Spencer, Herbert, 103, 150, 172; *An Autobiography,* 1, 4, 8, 11, 12, 52, 64, 115, 117–33, 153, 154, 155, 160, 161, 162, 163, 164, 180, 181, 182; *Biology,* 125; *Data of Ethics,* 125; *Descriptive Sociology,* 125, 126, 127; "The Development Hypothesis," 122; *Essays,* 129; *First Principles,* 124, 125; *Principles of Ethics,* 126; *Principles of Psychology,* 120, 123; *Principles of Sociology,* 126, 180; "Progress," 123; "The Proper Sphere of Government," 120; *Psychology,* 125; *Social Statics,* 120, 121, 122; "Style," 122; *Synthetic Philosophy,* 123, 125; "System of Philosophy," 124, 127; "A Theory of Population Deduced from the General Law of Animal Fertility," 122
Spencer, Thomas, 122, 124, 131
Spencer, William, 119, 125, 131
Spencer, William George (Spencer's father), 119, 120, 125, 127, 130, 131
Spengemann, William C., 169

Index

Spiritualism, 38, 39, 43, 44, 47, 48, 64
Sprigge, S. Squire, 107
Sprinker, Michael, 169
Spurzheim, Johann Kaspar, 42
Stanley, Henry Morton, 150, 154
Stanley, Liz, 178
Stillinger, Jack, 33, 37, 172, 174
Stockwell Grammar School, 109
Sunbury, 77
Super, R. H., 178
Svaglic, Martin J., 173
Symonds, J. A., 171

Tacitus, Publius Cornelius: *Life of Agricola*, 55
Taylor, Helen, 32, 174
Telford, Henry, 82
Tennyson, Alfred, Lord, 109
Textile industry: and the Industrial Revolution, 39, 40, 42, 43, 46, 47, 49
Thackeray, William Makepeace, 76, 114; *Henry Esmond*, 77
Thirty-nine Articles, 18, 112
Thwaite, Ann, 168, 182
Townsend, Francis G., 163, 184
Trollope, Anthony, 115; *An Autobiography*, 1, 2, 12, 57, 64, 69–79, 95, 100, 103, 107, 110, 113, 114, 121, 160, 162, 163, 164, 177, 178; *Barchester Towers*, 73; "Barsetshire series," 72; *The Last Chronicle of Barset*, 76; *The Macdermots of Ballycloran*, 73; "Palliser series," 72, 79; *The Prime Minister*, 71; *The Vicar of Bullhampton*, 76; *The Warden*, 73; *The Way We Live Now*, 71
Trollope, Frances (Trollope's mother), 71, 76, 78, 79
Trollope, Rose (Trollope's wife), 71
Trollope, Thomas Anthony (Trollope's father), 71
Turner, Jonathan H., 181
Turner, Joseph Mallord William, 83, 87

Unitarianism, 53, 55, 56, 64
Utilitarianism (Benthamism), 29, 30, 32, 35

Valéry, Paul: *La Jeune Parque*, 6
Vance, Eugene, 169
Veronese, Paul, 90
Victoria, Queen of England, 59
Virgil, 20, 138

Wallace, Alfred R., 99, 102
Ward, Mary Augusta (Mrs. Humphry): *A Writer's Recollections*, 9, 170, 171
Webster, Daniel, 58
Wedderburn, Alexander, 179
Wedgewood, Josiah, 97
Weintraub, Karl J., 173
Wesley, John, 139
Westminster Review, 29, 123
Whately, Richard, 16, 24
Wilson, James, 121
Winslow, Donald J., 167
Withers, Charlotte, 87
Woolf, James D., 182
Wordsworth, William, 29, 62, 163; *Essays upon Epitaphs*, 6; *The Prelude*, 4, 5, 33, 86, 170, 179
Wright, Frances, 38, 39, 42, 43

Young, Brigham, 75